INDUSTRIAL DEVELOPMENT

INDUSTRIAL DEVELOPMENT

Prof. M. Lakshmi Narasaiah
M.A., Ph.D.
&
K. Suresh
M.A., M. Phil.

Department of Economics
Sri Krishnadevaraya University,
Anantapur—515 003
(Andhra Pradesh)

DISCOVERY PUBLISHING HOUSE
NEW DELHI - 110 002

Published by :

Discovery Publishing House
4831/24, Ansari Road, Prahlad Street
Darya Ganj, New Delhi–110 002 (INDIA)
Phone : 327 9245
Fax : 91–11–3253475

First Published—1999

Reprinted-2011

ISBN 81–7141–464–8

L ser Typeset by :

Allied Computers,
Karnal (Haryana)

Printed at :

Mehra Offset Press, Delhi.

Preface

Industrialisation is 'sine-qua-non' for economic progress of any nation. Small-scale industrial occupy a place of vital importance in the process of economic development of India and have grown to prominence and registered phenomenal and spectacular growth over years through their multi-faceted contribution in terms of value added production, investment, foreign exchange earnings and employment generation. They are labour-intensive and need lesser investment. Their gestation period is also short. They generate more job opportunities and help in the dispersal of industries to backward areas giving way to balanced and rapid industrialisation.

Small-scale industries bring in to use the hitherto unexploited natural resources, strengthen and activate the otherwise stagnant economy and play a dominant role in converting the local raw resources in to value added commodities/services and also into more productive forms of capital. They stimulate production (agricultural and mineral) and add to national product, encourage savings, induce investment, promote capital formation, encourage expansion and diversification of production base, result in improvement of infrastructure facilities, tones up productive efficiency, augment technological innovation, research and development, bring into foreplay the hidden talents of skilled artisans, technicians and entrepreneurs and serve as propulsive factor in the process of economic development.

The development of small-scale industrial enterprises has been a movement in India and cumulatively these have grown to monumental size, contributing significantly to the value added production, investment, employment generation and exports. Recognising and realising their importance, the Government has been spending sizeable amounts through the quin-quennial plans for the development of this sector.

Today there are more than two million Small-scale Industrial Units in India, the largest number in any single country in the world. They account for 35 per cent of India's overall industrial production and 30 per cent of India's export earnings. With investment around Rs. 18,200 crores, production of the value of Rs. 1,80,000 crores and exports around Rs. 9,700 crores, and providing employment to around 120 lakh people-Small-Scale Industrial units are the crux of Indian industrial development.

Finance is regarded as the potential power and life-blood of any industrial enterprise irrespective of the fact whether it is small, medium or large. It is the master-key which provides access to all the vital inputs which are indispensable for any business/industrial activity.

Finance is to business what blood is to human body. But in the human body mechanism, there is to a greater extent, an automatic regulation of flow of blood. No such automation is available in case of any industrial enterprise to regulate the flow of this money-blood. It is to be managed carefully by able, skilled and competent person(s).

To improve the financial position of these units, some of the financial institutions such as Industrial Development Bank of India, Andhra Pradesh Industrial Development Corporation, Andhra Pradesh Small-scale Industries Development Corporation, Andhra Pradesh State Financial Corporation and other commercial banks have been financing the small-scale industrial sector. Of all these financial institutions Andhra Pradesh State Financial Corporation stands as one of the major financial contributors to this sector. Hence, this study is centralised on the corporation.

The present study is an earnest attempt to find how the management of finance is done in the Small-scale Industrial Units in Anantapur district of Andhra Pradesh. Andhra Pradesh constitutes three regions : (1) Coastal Andhra (2) Telengana and (3) Rayalaseema. Rayalaseema region, which was once an abode of sparkling splendour, is now a synonym for drought and poverty. It is a typical dry tract in Andhra Pradesh, with inadequate and uncertain rainfall, inhospitable soil, vast stretches of barren land purctuated by huge boulders and hillocks. Of the four districts that constitute Rayalaseema, Anantapur is one, the other three being Cuddapah, Kurnool and Chittoor of these four district.

Authors

Contents

1

Introduction

Need for Industrialisation in India

Developing economy like India should change from a sellers' to a buyers' market as short-ages of goods have disappeared to satisfy the human wants resulting in higher per capita income. But the gap in per capita incomes between the developed and under-developed countries in largely reflected in the disparity in the structure of their economies. The former are largely industrial economies, while in the latter production is confined predominantly to agriculture. Table 1.1 clearly reveals the positive relationship between per capita income and the share of manufacturing output (industry including constructions).

Evidently, industrialisation has a major role to play in the economic development of developing countries like India. The essential precondition for breaking vicious circle and accelerating development is a major shift from low productivity occupations to high productivity occupations. In general, the net value of output per person is higher industry than in agriculture. In industry the scope for internal as well as external economies is greater than in other sectors

Table 1.1

Country	*Per capita income (in U.S. $)*	*Industrial origin of G.D.P. at factor cost (Percentage)*		
		Agri-culture	*Indus-try*	*Servi-ces*
U.S.A.	14,110	2	32	66
Canada	12,310	3	29	68
Belgium	9,150	2	35	63
U.K.	9,200	2	32	66
Japan	10,120	4	42	54
Phillippines	760	22	36	42
India	270	36	28	38

Source : World Bank, *World Development Report, 1985.*

and certainly greater than in agriculture. As industrialisation proceeds, economies of scale and inter-industrial linkages become more pronounced. It also leads to the creation of economic surplus in the hands of industrial producers for further investment. Industrialisation acts as in instrument both for creating capacity to absorb excess labour power and for creating an environment for diversification of the market required at higher stages of economic development.

In the words of Myrdal, industrialisation is held to be crucial to develop a strategy because it will radiate stimuli throughout the economy of the country and lift it out of stagnation and poverty. Thus, industrialisation can serve as an effective instrument to uplift the socio; economic conditions of the people[1].

Industrial sector which possesses a relatively high marginal propensity to save and invest contributes significantly to the eventual achievement of a self-sustaining economy with continued high levels of investment and rapid rate of increase in income and industrial employment. It means that if only when India has acquired the ability to design, fabricate and erect its own plants without foreign assistance that it will become a truly advanced and industrialised country[2].

It is thus clear that industrialisation is a pre-requisite for raising national income as well as per capita income, to remove unemployment and underemployment, to promote agriculture which helps to accelerate the pace of economic progress.

Significance of Small–Scale Industries

The contribution of small-scale industries to industrial development and economic development is a multiple one. The development of small-scale industries is not only crucial for accelerating industrial growth both also for achieving the social objectives of dispersal of industry and equitable distribution of wealth. The small industries will certainly encourage the new class of entrepreneurs, particularly the uneducated unemployed, to start their industrial ventures.

The small-scale industries enjoy the unique position in the process of rural transformation of less developed countries like India with nearly 80 percent of the population living in rural areas and very large proportion unemployed or underemployed. So the development of small-scale industries is a programme requiring not only immediate attention but quick implementation on a fairly large scale.

Strategy of Small Industry in India

The programme for the development of small industries has been accorded a high place in India. Ever since the days of Gandhiji, the small industry movement has been largely regarded as a vehicle for uplifting the weaker sections of the population. After independence, when the problem of regional imbalances began to appear, small industry was considered as the natural vehicle for redressing such imbalances. More recently, when the problem of unemployment has began to take an acute form, the ability of the small industry to provide jobs at a comparatively lower cost became an attractive proposition for the planner and the administration.

Organisation

In India, small industry development is the concern of the Ministry of Industrial Development through the Development Commissioner (Small-scale industries). Set up in 1954, the Central Small Industries Organisation has grown to a vast network of about 25 small industries service institutes, 20 branch institutes and 41 extension centres spread through out the country[3]. The Small Industries Development Organisation (SIDO), as it is now called, consists of specialised institutions dealing with the specific area such as instrumentation, Tool Design and a network of tool rooms as well as test centres setup in various parts of the country to provide specialised facilities to small industrial units, making it the largest promotion agency of its kinds in the world. Associated with the small industry development organisation, are the National Small Industries Corporation (NSIC), which is operated as a public sector undertaking, and a small Industries Extension Training Institute (SIET) at Hyderabad which is the main centre for training personnel connected with small industry.[4]

At the national level, in addition to the Small Industries Development Organisation, there are organisations dealing with handlooms, headed by Development Commissioner (handlooms), and handicrafts headed by similar officials. In addition, a statutory body-Khadi* and 23 other designated Village Industries, and operates a large number of schemes for the growth and development of those industries. While the small industry development organisation is with Ministry of Industry, the handlooms and handicrafts are dealt with by the Ministry of Commerce. There are separate boards dealing with specific product such as coir and silk, both of which have tremendous potential for growth in the rural areas.

At the state level, the problem is much less since many of the areas are dealt with by the Director (or Commissioners)

* The expression 'Khadi' refers to handspun and hand-woven cloth popularised by Gandhiji during the freedom struggle.

of industry operating at the State level assisted by the Small Industries Development Corporations set up in every state.

At the district level, District Industries Centres have been set up in most of the districts to cater to the growth of the industries in the region.

At the block level, with a population of approximately 1,00,000 people, rural industry is part of an integrated programme of rural development. Attempts are now being made to develop greater linkages between industry and the main stream of rural development.[5]

Definitions

At one time, the Government grouped small-scale industrial undertakings into two categories—those using power but employing less than 50 persons, and those not using power but employing less than 100 persons.

Now it is seen that the definition of small industry in India is primarily confined to capital investments and does not take into account the number employed or the location.

In March, 1985, the Government has defined small-sale enterprises as undertakings with a fixed capital investment in plant and machinery about Rs. 20 lakhs to Rs. 35 lakhs and for ancillary units from Rs. 25 lakhs to Rs. 45 lakhs.

Financial Support

In India, credit for the small-scale sector is provided primarily by the State Financial Corporations for medium term loans and through commercial banks for working capital. Various State Governments also provide loans of small amount upto Rs. 1,00,000 under the State Aid to Industries Act. Concessional finance is provided by the financial institutions to the small-scale sector and in respect of loans below Rs. 25,000 no collateral is insisted upon. In practice, however, the problem of obtaining finances becomes increasingly acute as the size of the unit becomes smaller. A National Bank for

Rural Development has been set-up recently to provide, amongst other things, funds for small industries in rural areas.

Technology

Regional testing centres have been set-up under the Small Industrial Development Organisation while a few prototype Development and Training Centres (PTC) are being operated by the *NSIC*. In addition, process and product development centres are proposed to be set-up at locations and in fields relevant to the small-scale sector.

Marketing

In India, marketing has always been a major problem for the small industrial units although significant increase in exports is being registered. Small units suffer from lack of up-to-date market information and ability to make frequent visits abroad to contact potential customers. Even within the country, small units find it difficult to compete with large companies, particularly in respect of consumer goods where 'brand consciousness' is an important criterion. Government has provided specific support programmes such as purchase and preference policy; but this has provided a limited assistance to the small-scale units, as seen by the fact that the share of the small units even in Government purchases is still below 15 percent. The problem is likely to become even more acute as small industrial units get established outside the metropolitan areas. The question of organisational support, which needs to be provided to the small units so as to make them able to compete on, equal terms with the large units, is under consideration by the Government.

Modernisation

In India, modernisation of the small-scale industry has been considered since the late sixties when a Government committee identified five industries-machine tools, automobile ancillaries, domestic, electrical appliances, foundry and hosiery-as being ripe for modernisation. Subsequently, more industries have been added to the lists; and the small industries service institutes operate a programme of modernisation under which studies are conducted to indicate the specific manner in which modernisation can be done. The basic weakness of the programme has been the lack of funds on soft terms to finance such improvements. However, the Industrial Development Bank of India is working on a plant to provide such funds and it is expected that once such a plan is implemented, the programme of modernisation may gather momentum.

Sickness in Industry

The problem of industrial sickness figures prominently in India where there is a considerable publicity on the incidence of sickness among units. However, an estimate made by the Reserve Bank of India has shown that a little more than 20,000 units are reported to be sick out of a total number of 600,00 units registered with it. If this is correct, the percentage of sick units works out to 3 percent which cannot be considered as unduly high. The basic problem is to identify genuine sick units which could be rehabilitated and to undertake a co-ordinated programme for such rehabilitation. A sick units Committee operates in each state but its efforts have been hampered by lack of adequate funds to be provided to the sick units. In some states, the State Financial Corporations have taken the lead in doing so and Governments are considering to provide more credit for units.

Industrial Policies and Small-Scale Industries

A study of the industrial policy documents reveals that small-scale industry has been assigned an important role throughout the period since India's independence. Thus, for example, protection and promotion of small-scale industry has all along been listed as a major objective in all of the industrial policy documents. The policy statements also indicate the lines on which the Government has been taking or contemplating concrete steps.

The points may be highlighted by referring to the industrial policy resolutions.

Industrial Policy Resolution of 1948

The Industrial Policy Resolution of 1948 states that the small-scale industries are particularly suited for better utilisation of local resources and for the achievement of self-sufficiency in respect of certain types of essential consumer goods. It is also recognised that the healthy expansion of small-scale industries depends upon the factors like adequate provision of raw materials, cheap power, technical advice, organised marketing of their products where necessary, safeguards against intensive competition from large-scale manufactures and the education of workers in the use of best available resources.[6]

Industrial Policy Resolution of 1956

The resolution states that the small industries provide immediate large-scale employment, they offer a method of ensuring more equitable distribution of national income and they facilitated an effective mobilisation of resources of capital and skills which might otherwise have remained unutilised. Further, it adds that the decentralised sector should acquire sufficient vitality to be self-supporting and its development be integrated with that of large-scale industries. The state will, therefore, concentrate on measures designed to improve the competitive strength of the small producers.[7]

Industrial Policy Resolution of 1977

This resolution has placed maximum importance for the development of small-scale industries and it may be called as "Small-scale Industrial Policy 1977". The statement envisages that "whatever can be produced by small-scale and cottage industries must only be so produced". The list of items produced by small industry would be extensively reserved for small-scale sector has been sufficiently expanded.[8] While reserving 504 items exclusively for small-scale industry, the

Government has also considered special legislation in order to protect the interests of cottage and small-scale households, industries with a view to ensure that these activities which provide self-employment in large number get due recognition in industrial development. It is also proposed to set-up District Industries Centres (DICs) to enable the small entrepreneurs to have all kinds of services under the same roof.[9]

Industrial Policy Resolution, 1980

The industrial policy statement made by Government of India on 23rd July, 1980 primarily seeks to harmonise the growth in the small-scale sector with the large and medium sectors. The emphasis in the new policy is on fostering the complementarity between large and small sector so that the new dichotomies (which are more apparent that real) between the two sectors do not distort the economic pattern.

The salient features of the new industrial policies concerning small-scale industries is the increase of investment limit of small industries. The Government decided—

1) to increase the limit of investment in case of tiny units from Rs. 1 lakh to Rs. 2 lakhs

2) to increase the limit of investment in case of small-scale units from Rs. 10 lakhs to 20 lakhs and

3) to increase the limit of investment in case of ancillaries from Rs. 15 lakhs to 25 lakhs[10]

In view of the escalations in the cost of plant and machinery since 1980 when the investment limits were fixed, the Government has decided to redefine the small-scale industry as a unit engaged in processing, manufacturing, preserving and servicing activity with investment in plant and machinery (excluding investment for research and development purpose) not exceeding Rs. 35 lakhs, Besides this, tiny units are those industrial units which are situated in an area with a population not exceeding 50,000 (according to 1971 census), investment in plant and machinery not more than Rs. 2 lakhs per unit which are locally available raw-material and sell their products in local markets. Ancillary units are those small industries which supply atleast 50 per cent of their products to some of the big industrial units and for them the investment in plant and machinery may be upto Rs. 45 lakhs.[11]

Owing to all-round efforts made by the Government through its industrial policy resolutions and liberalised licensing policy, there is a tremendous increase in number of small-scale industries. Table 1.2 clearly exhibits the growth of small-scale industries, its importance in providing employment opportunities and its share in the total production of industrial produce and exports.

Development of Small-Scale Industries During Plan Period

Till independence, only cottage industries, village industries, rural industries or agro-based industries were considered to be small industries. The National Planning Committee, set up in 1938 under the Chairmanship of Pandit Jawaharlal Nehru, constituted a panel to study this problem. With the down of planned era in the country, the Government has been following a policy of promotion as well as protection of the small industries sector, but the protection would be gradually reduced as and when promotional activities begin to produce results.

The state of affairs in which small-scale industries were at that time was well described in the First Plan document as "there have been hardly any considered and co-ordinated programmes of development and technical improvement, and great deal of small industry has grown up without much direction and assistance from the Government.[12] In the Second Plan, a number of new programmes were organised and steps were taken to provide a more assured market for the products of the some of the industries. And also it

Table 1.2 : Growth Parameters Pertaining to Small-scale Industries

Variables	*1975–76*	*1980–81*	*1981–82*	*1982–83*	*1983–84*	*1984–85*	*1989–90*
No. of Registered Units (cumulative in lakhs)	2.46	4.48	5.23	6.03	6.79	8.00	10.00
Value of output (including in registered units) (Rs. in crores)	11,000	28,660	32,600	35,000	41,620	50,520	50,520
Employment (including un-registered Units) (in lakhs)	44	71	75	79	84	89	109
Exports (In crores) Exports as percentage of	637	1,643	2,070	2,100	2,350	2,580	4,140
Value of Output	5.8	5.9	6.4	6.0	4.7	5.1	5.2

Source : *Annual Reports*, Union Ministry of Industries and *VII Five Year Plan* (The Hindu, *The Survey of Indian Industries, 1985, p. 253*).

stressed the need for a "co-ordinated policy based on close collaboration between the Reserve Bank, the State Bank of India, the State Finance Corporation and the Central Co-operative Banks.[13] The total outlay on small-scale industries in the Second Plan was Rs. 180 crores as against Rs. 43 crores in the First Plan. In the Third Five Year Plan, among the developments in the field of small-scale industries proposed, a reference may be made to the development of depots for stocking raw materials which are in short supply to be made available to small units with a view to assisting in the fuller utilisation of existing capacity. Two of the main objectives of the Third Plan in regard to the programme for village and small-scale industries are

1) to promote the growth of industries in rural areas and in small towns;

2) to promote the development of small-scale industries as ancillaries to large industries.[14]

An outlay of Rs. 241 crores had been made in the public sector for small industries. In addition, Rs. 273 crores were expected to be invested from private sources including financial institutions. The Fourth Five Year Plan document outlined that the main aim of the development programmes for small-scale industries was fuller utilisation of the capacity already established, interim development of selected industries including ancillaries and industrial co-operative and subject to the criteria of feasibility, promotion of industries in semi-urban, urban and backward areas.[15] The broad strategy proposed to be followed in the Fifth Five Year Plan was to entail a considerable enlargement of the development programmes for providing assistance and facilities in various forms to these industries.[16] Both Sixth Plan and Seventh Plan mark a significant stage in the development of small-scale industries in the context of the national development strategy aiming at improvement in the levels of production and earnings, creation of additional employment opportunities on dispersed and decentralised basis. Thus it is evident that laid the emphasis on the development of small-scale industries has been increasing in the successive five year plans. A well-known researcher on small industry commented that India has, by all odds, the largest most comprehensive and the best planned programme for small industry development.[17] At this stage, It is an appropriate to recall the words of a noble laureate, about the stress of Indian Plans on small-scale industry. "As early as in the First Five Year Plan, the promotion of small-scale industry acquired the status of a public policy objective and in later rounds of planning, it was given more and more stress".[18]

In tune with the broad lines of industrial policy resolution and specific steps proposed in successive five year plans, a number of incentive and financial assistance programmes have been formulated for small industry growth.

Financial Problems of Small-Scale Sector

One of the main hurdles confronting the growth of small-scale industries in India is lack of adequate finance. The non-availability of credit on easy terms has been the major handicap of these industries. Though the Government of India and the financing institutions have introduced various schemes to assist these industries in providing credit facilities, the problem still seems to be chronic. In the words of Alexander " among all the problems faced by small industries, absence of credit facilities has been the most serious one.[19] Another mentioned that the existing agencies including banks have not been able to meet the needs of the situation.[20]

In one of the reports it was pointed out that the special feature of the banking system in India has been its security-oriented approach instead of development-oriented approach which is essential for accelerating industrial growth in a developed country.[21] Due to this the financing agencies are shy often hesitant in meeting the genuine needs of bonafide small-scale industrial enterprises.[22] Some other changes turned against the financing agencies are that they are security-minded and the entrepreneur has to spent a lots of time and money, as he has to wade through a lot of forms, rules, regulations and has to pay bribes.[23]

It is ironical that small-scale industrial sector which now contributes more than 40 percent of the industrial output, has been provided with just only 11 percent of the total credit sanctioned by commercial banks.[24] Even now many small industrial units are depending on non-institutional sources for their financial requirements. Mathur feels that adequate finance is pure pre-requisite for proper organisation of production and the purchase of raw materials, investment of capital in manufacture and the ultimate profit from the venture.[25]

The Role of Financial Institutions

The availability of finance might be the most important determinant in the establishment and growth of small manufacturing enterprises. This observation has not been confined only to under-developed regions but is equally true for countries with very different cultural and institutional backgrounds and also with the various levels of industrialisations. Metaphorically, finance is the lubricant of the process of economic growth.[26] When finance becomes available, industrial development is initiated and new investment opportunities arise. The newly developed access to funds on reasonable terms induces or encourages entrepreneurs to expand their horizon of conceivable opportunities. Not simply access to funds but the entire financial milien and the rationalism it implies triggers creative entrepreneurial responses.[27] The supply of this finance has to be canalized through specialised financial and developmental institutions which act as pump-primers rather than conduit for the factors of production.[28]

The welfare objective enshrined in our constitution implied that in any pattern of development, the small man's welfare was to be given a high priority. Small industries, with large employment potential requiring comparatively small capital and being capable of dispersal, provide an obvious answer. It was accepted that they had a distinct role to play in the socio-economic uplift of the people.[29] But the entrepreneurs who thrive in certain types of environment, get shifted in others and unless the environment is propitious, enterprise is sporadic and feeble.[30] Hence there was a need for radical transformation of the whole environment so as to make it conducive to widespread entrepreneurship. This role of development finance supplied through specialised institutional agencies has been regarded to the vital in this regard.[31] However, one should remember that development finances was only one tool, through a powerful one.[32]

Recognising the need for specialised financial and developmental institutions, the Government of India and the State Governments immediately after attaining political freedom, set on the task of building up a network of such institutions. The different institutions that extend financial assistance are as follow :

1) Andhra Pradesh Small-Scale Industrial Development Corporation (APSSIDC)

2) Andhra Pradesh State Financial Corporation (APSFC)

3) Andhra Pradesh Industrial Infrastructure Corporation (APIIC)

Statement of the Problem

So far many attempts have been made to study the various problems that are facing by the Small-Scale Industries in various aspects such as marketing problem, raw material problem, labour problem etc. by various research scholars and others. But little is contributed towards the financial problems that are facing by small scale industry. In this study Andhra Pradesh State Financial Corporation which is one of the major financing body for small Scale Industries, is studied. This study is a regional study concentrating on Anantapur district. It is hoped that the study will throw light on this problem.

Need of the Study

Financial problem is one of the important problems of small-scale industry. To improve the financial position of these units, some of the financial institutions such as Industrial Development Bank of India, Andhra Pradesh Industrial Development Corporation, Andhra Pradesh Small-Scale Industries Development Corporation, Andhra Pradesh State Financial Corporation and other commercial banks have been financing the small scale industrial sector. Of all these financial institutions Andhra Pradesh State Financial Corporation stands as one of the major financial contributors to this sector. Hence, this study is centralised on the Corporation.

This book aims

1) To study the development of Small-Scale Industry.
2) To study the performance of Andhra Pradesh State Financial Corporation.
3) To review the financial assistance of Andhra Pradesh State Financial Corporation to Small-Scale Industries in Andhra Pradesh State.
4) To study the role of Andhra Pradesh State Financial Corporation in financing Small-Scale Industries in Anantapur district.

Notes :

1. Gunnar Myrdal : Asian drama, *An inquiry into the poverty of the Nations* (London : the twentieth century Fund, inc., 1968) p. 1150.
2. Ruddar Dutt and K.P.M. Sundaram : *Indian Economy*, S. Chand & Company (Pvt.) Limited; New Delhi, 1989, p. 525.
3. *Small Industry Bulletin for Asia and the Pacific No. : 19*—United Nations, New York, 1984, p. 2.

4. Ibid.
5. Ibid.
6. Industrial Policy: 1948—Government of India, Industrial Policy Resolution dated 6th April, 1948. As cited by Ram. K. Vepa, *Small Industries in Seventies*, New Delhi, Vikas Publishing House, 1971.
7. Industrial Policy : 1956—Govt. of India, Industrial Policy Resolution of 1956, *Programmes of Industrial Development*, 1956–61 (New Delhi : 1956) p. 432.
8. Industrial Policy : 1977—Govt. of India, Planning Commission, *Draft VIth Five Year Plan* Revised (1978–83), New Delhi, 1978, p. 379.
9. Govt. of India, Industrial Policy Resolution, dated 23rd December, 1977.
10. Industrial Policy 1980 : *Financial Express* (daily), July 24th (New Delhi edition).
11. *Employment News*, Delhi, Vol. XI, No. : 25, 20th September, 1986, p. 1.
12. Govt. of India : *First Five Year Plan*, Planning Commission (New Delhi), 1952, p. 326.
13. Govt. of India : *Second Five Year Plan*, Planning Commission, New Delhi, 1956, p. 440.
14. Govt. of India : *Third Five Year Plan*, Planning Commission (New Delhi), 1960, p. 426.
15. Govt. of India : *Fourth Five Year Plan*, Planning Commission (New Delhi), 1969, p. 29.
16. Govt. of India : *Fifth Five Year Plan*, Planning Commission (New Delhi), 1974, p. 34.
17. Eugence Staly : "Productive Development of Small Industry", *Productivity* (Vol. 3, No. 56, Aug.–Sep.–Oct., 1962, p. 83.4.
18. Gunnar Myrdal : *Asian Drama—An Enquiry into the Poverty of Nations*, Vol. II, London, 20th Century Fund, Inc., 1968, p. 1227.
19. P.C. Alexander : *Industrial Estates in India*. (Bombay : Asia Publishing House, 1963) p. 3.
20. R.V. Rao : *Small Industries and the Developing Economy in India*, (New Delhi : Concept Publishing Company, 1979), p. 128.
21. National Alliance of Young Entrepreneurs : Study on credit facilities for small-scale industries in India and abroad. *Economic Trends* (Vol. VII No. 22, 16th Nov., 1979) p. 5.

22. *Ibid.* 0.5.

23. Indira Gidwani : "Plight of Small Industry"—*Economic Times* dated 11th July, 1977.

24. Gopal Swaroop : *Advances to Small Industries and Small Borrowers* (New Delhi, Sultan Chand & Sons, 1970), p. 5.

25. S.P. Mathur: *Economics of Small-scale Industries* (Delhi–Sundeep Prakashan, 1979), p. 129.

26. Rondo Camaron and Hugh T. Patrick : "Introduction", Banking in Early States of Industrialisation, A Study in Comparative Economic History, Rondo Cameron (New York : Oxford University Press, 1967), p. 2.

27. Hugh T. Patrick : "Financial Development and Economic Growth in Underdeveloped Countries". *Economic Development and Cultural Change* (Vol. 19, No. : 3. 1971) p. 467.

28. William Diamond : *Development Banks* (Baltimore : The Hopkins Press, 1957), p. 4.

29. M.C. Sharkar : "Financing the New Entrepreneurs", *State Bank of India Monthly Review.* (Vol. XIII, No. 6, June 1974) p. 210.

30. P.S. Lokanatham : "Entrepreneurship : Supply of Entrepreneurs and Technologiests with special reference to India". *Economic Development with special reference to East Asia.* Proceedings of a conference held by the international Economic Association, ed., Kenneth Beril (London : Maxmillan & Company Ltd., 1965), p. 165.

31. R.A. Sharma : "Entrepreneurial Motivation in India". The review of Commerce Studies (Vol. III, 1974), pp. 26.33.

32. Robert W. Deverport : *Financing the Small Manufacture in Developing Countries* (New York : Megvaw Mill Book Co., 1967) pp. 10–11.

2

The Profile of Anantapur District

Historical Background

Anantapur, geographically, is the largest district of Andhra Pradesh. The district was formed in the year 1882 after its separation from Bellary district. Later on the boundaries of the district were extended with the inclusion of: Kadiri taluk of Cudapah district in 1910 and Rayadrug taluk of Bellary district in 1956. With all these, the area of the district is 19,125 sq. kms.[1]

Physical Features

It lies western most in Andhra Pradesh state, between 13 Deg 40 Min and 15 Deg 15 Min Northern latitude and 76 Deg 50Min and 78 Deg 30 Min eastern longitude.[2] The district is bounded by Kurnool district on the North, Cuddapah district on the East and Bangalore and Chitradurga District on the N.H. 7 about 360 km. from the state capital Hyderabad. The district comprises of 3 Revenue Divisions, viz. Anantapur, Dharmavaram and Penukonda. These division are divided in to 63 Mandals.

Natural Divisions of the District

The district can be roughly divided into three natural regions-the northern, the central and the southern. Uravakonda, Gooty and Tadipatri taluks form the northern region; a large part of it is black cotton soil. Anantapur, Kalyandrug, Rayadrug, Dharmavarm, Kadiri and Penukonda taluks constitute the Central region and Central part of the district, while Madakasira and Hindupur Taluks constitute the southern region which is higher is elevation than the rest of the district. Both the central and the southern regions are largely of red soil.

Climate

82% of the soils in the district consists of Red Soil and 18% Black soil. The variation in the climatic conditions is large between summer Maximum temperature which tudes 42 Deg. Centigrade in the months of April and May and the Lowest Temperature of 16 Deg. Centigrade in winter months of December and January. The average rainfall is 555 mm.

Humidity

The period from February to May is the driest part of the year, when the relative humidity is 50-60 per cent in the mornings and 20-30 per cent in the afternoons. It goes up during the southwest monsoon and retreating monsoon seasons.

Rainfall

In 1981 the annual rainfall in the district was 544 mm. as against 672 mm. and 896 mm. for the Rayalaseema region*

* Rayalaseema forms one of the three natural divisions of regions oı Andhra Pradesh. It consists of four districts viz., Anantapur, Cuddapah, Chittoor and Kurnool. These districts were ceded to the British by the Nizam of Hyderabad in the 18th century in return for military help and protection. Therefore, the districts of Rayalaseema were known as 'Ceded Districts'. From the 3rd decade of this century, the Ceded districts came to be known as 'Rayalaseema' (or the hand of Krishnadevaraya).

and Andhra Pradesh respectively[3]. The rainfall in the district is not only scanty but uneven and uncertain with a high coefficient of variation (CV). This rainfall is insufficient for raising any crop successfully. Wells, bore-wells, tanks and canals form the chief sources of water for cultivation.

Since Anantapur district is located in the centre of the Southern peninsula, the south-west monsoons are prevented from western ghats; and the north-west monsoons cannot penetrate, because of its distance from the Bay of Bengal. Thus, the district accounts for the lowest rainfall in the state.

Ground Water Potential

As per the estimates given by the State Ground Water Department, the total groundwater reserves has been indicated to be of the order of 1,76,343 hectare meters for the Anantapur district. The present level of utilisation has been estimated at 57,020 hectare meters, leaving a balance of 1,19,323 hectare meters for further development in the Anantapur district. The availability of Groundwater is at the depth of approximately 100 feet.

Rivers in the District

The chief river of Anantapur is the Pennar which is not a perennial stream but comes down in freshes for short periods, specially, during the rainy season, thereafter, except for small trickle in the middle of its sandy bed dries up again almost at once. Chitravathi is another river of some significance in this district. The Hagari river which with its tributary, Chinna Hagari river, runs right through the heart of the Rayadrug taluk, is another important river of this district. Bhayaravanthippa project, constructed across this river provides irrigation facilities to Rayadrug and Kalyandrug taluks. Apart from these, streams like Kushavathi, Swaranmukhi, Tadakaleru, Pandemeru, Mandaleru are the other sources of water to various large and small irrigations tanks of this district. All the above said rivers and streams flow only during the rainy season. Thus, there are no perennial sources of water in the district.

Power

For meeting the demands of domestic and industrial power requirements in the district power is drawn mainly from the Thungabhadra Hydro Electric station at Hospet, through a distribution network. There is a 66 Kv single circuit line from Gooty to Hindupur touching Kallur, Dharmavaram and Penukonda. A 33 Kv single circuit line from Gooty to Hindupur touching Kallur, Dharmavaram and Penukonda. A 33 Kv Single circuit line is passing from Obulapuram to Kalyandrug via Rayadrug. A 33 Kv line in existence between Hindupur and Jammalabanda, Dharamavaram and Narpala, and Mudigubba and Kadiri. A 56 KV circuit line laid between Gooty and Bellary, via Guntakal. Another 56 Kv double circuit line laid from Gooty to Kurnool and a 132 Kv single circuit line from Gooty to Dharamavaram also exists.

Transport and Communication

The district is very well connected through National High ways and Railways to all the cosmopolitan cities of the India to facilitate the raw material and market tie up network.

In addition to a T.V. relay Station, there are 4 Head Post Offices 108 Sub post offices and 782 branch post offices besides 86 telegraph offices including combined offices.

Live Stock

The district is considered rich in live-stock. The particulars of live-stock relating to 1981 census are given in the Table 2.1.

The estimated availability of the bone is around 3,000 tonnes approximately and offers a good scope of industrial use. There are two units established producing yearly 200 tonnes of bone meal a year.

The estimate of the wool production is around 200 Metric tonnes and about 10,000 rural artisans are engaged in the weaving of cumblies etc., There is a good scope for

Table 2.1 : The Livestock Wealth of the District

S.No.	*Name of Animal*	*No. of Animal*
1.	White Cattle	6,64,581
2.	Black Cattle	2,89,319
3.	Sheep	7,54,837
4.	Goat	3,72,508
5.	Pigs	25,301
6.	Poultry	6,78,739
7.	Horses and Ponies	1,468
8.	Donkies	15,423
9.	Ducks	1,024

Source : Government of Andhra Pradesh, *Department of Industries, Action Plan, 1983–84 to 1989–90*, for Industrial Development in Anantapur District. p. 13.

setting up a mechanised wool carding, dyeing, and woolen blanket weaving units.

Human Resources in the Anantapur District

The total population of the District is 25.48 lakhs according to 1981 census comprising of 20.16 lakhs (79.12%) rural and 5.32 lakhs (20.88%) urban population. The district is less densely populated with a density of population 133 per sq. km. as against 196 for the sate, as a whole of the total population 42.25 percent are workers, while 57.75% are non workers. Out of the workers 40.82 percent constitute cultivators, 34.57% constitute agricultural labourers and 24.6% other workers including 4.2 percent working in the household sector in the District [4]. Thus, 75.4 per cent of the workers are dependent on agriculture. Among the Rayalaseema districts, this district has the largest percentage of workers to the total population [5]. The number of inhabited villages are 934, while that of uninhabited villages 28.

Position of Educated Unemployed as on 31 May, 1988

The Table 2.2 reveals the following facts.

Table 2.2 : Detailed Position of Educated Unemployed as on 31st May, 1988

Category	*Total*	*S.C.*	*S.T.*	*B.C.*	*Others*
Graduates	6658	70	7	728	5853
L.C.E.	433	25	2	74	332
L.M.E.	215	8	1	25	177
L.E.E.	247	4	0	1	232
Other Diploma Holders (LECE, LAE, Etc.)	87	3	0	5	79
B.Ed.	1623	16	2	188	1407
ITI	488	24	6	101	257
I.T.I.	2744	234	41	392	2077
Under Graduate	50145	1583	413	8217	39932
Steno Typist	180	14	02	18	146
Typist	2177	56	26	634	1461
Other Educated Applicants like Telugu, Hindi Pandits & B.Ed. Teachers	12074	1393	253	3770	6649
Uneducated Applicants Cooks & Light Vehicle Drivers	39681	10283	1424	11179	1645

Note : FC = Forward Castes; BC = Backward Castes;
SC = Scheduled Castes; ST = Scheduled Tribes

Source : Office of the Employment Exchange, Anatapur

i) **Graduates** : There are 6658 graduates in the live register of the Employment Exchange of Anantapur district which includes 70 S.C's., 7 S.T.'s and 728 B.C.'s.

ii) **Under Graduates** : There are 50,145 under graduates which includes 1,583 SC's, 413 ST's and 8,217 BC.s in the live register of the Employment Exchange of Anantapur district.

iii) **Degree/Diploma Holders in Engineering & Technical Disciplines :** There are 433 LCE, 215 LME, 247 LEE and 87 other diploma holders and also 2,744 ITI trained candidates in the live register of the Employment Exchange of Anantapur district.

Educational Infrastructure

A unique feature of the district is that it has 2 universities viz. Sri Krishna Devaraya University, Anantapur and Sri Satyasaibaba Institute of Higher Learning, Puttaparthi besides on Oil Technological Research Institute attached to JNTU including a Dry Farm Agricultural Research station of APAU exist in the district. In addition to the above the district consists of one JNTU College of Engineering, 2 Polytechnic Colleges, 13 Degree Colleges, 28 Junior Colleges 258 High Schools and 2 I.T.I. Institutions. The percentage of literate persons in 1981 was 28.68 as against 30 and 36 for the state and the country[6].

The Table 2.3 gives a picture of educational institutional that are rendering services to the people in the district.

Mineral Wealth

Anantapur district is well known for its mineral resources especially for its gold and diamond deposits. Thus, steatite, which cuddapah does not produce and gold, which is mined neither in Cuddapah and Kurnool are fond in this district at Ramagiri on a substantial Scale[7]. The other important minerals are lime stone, dolomite, asbestos, barytes, iron ores, corundum, steatite, clay, white shale, turpentine, green quartz, dimension and building stones. There are 137 mining leases existing in the district covering an extent of 10,941 acres.

Black, pink and Multi coloured granites are available in the district, which are used in the cutting and polishing industry.

Table 2.3 : Details of the Educational Institutions in Anantapur District

S.No.	Type of Institution	No. of Institutions	No. of Students
1.	Primary Schools	2,406	2,45,189
2.	Upper Primary Schools	138	31,609
3.	High Schools	213	80,048
4.	Junior Colleges	29	9,437
5.	Degree Colleges	13	9,039
6.	Polytechnic Colleges :		
	a) Polytechnic College for boys & girls at Anantapur	1	347
	b) Polytechnic College for girls at Hindupur	1	120
7.	Technical School	1	198
8.	Industrial Training Institutions	2	.....
9.	Engineering College	1	839
10.	Universities :		
	1. Sri Krishnadevaraya University Anantapur	1	.....
	2. Sri Satya Sai Institute of Higher Learning—A deemed University	1	.....

Source : Data News Feature, *Andhra Pradesh Year Book*, 1989, Hyderabad, p. 158.

The Table 2.4 gives the details relating to the different types of minerals, their position and place of occurrence. It explains that most of the minerals viz., barytes, limestones, steatite, white clay, taleum and asbestos are available in Tadipatri taluk of the district.

Financial Resources

There are 202 bank branches in the district. Syndicate Bank is the lead bank. There are 17 financial institutions operating in the district. Andhra Pradesh State Finance Corporation is the major term lending institution. Rs. 12.56

Table 2.4 : Mineral Potential

Sl. No.	*Name of Mineral*	*Localities*	*Estimated Reserves (in tonnes)*
1.	Asbestos	Vanganpalli Singeraguttapalli Jelakalva	2,50,000 for both Cuddapah and Anantapur district.
2.	Barytes	Ellutle, Venkatapalli	77,000
3.	Clays	Balapuram	1,000
4.	Gold	Ramagiri Yepamana mines	Proved reserves 0.2 million tonnes with 6–7 gm./tonne grade for 100 m depth
5.	Diamond	Om pratime– Ganglappa-Section Wajrakaruru, Ganjikunta, Lattavaram, Konganapalli	Not Available
6.	High Grade Limestone	Rayalacheruvu Kona-uppalapadu	1.5 million 2,00,000
7.	Iron-ore	Sidhapuram Obulapuram Melanpannengudi	1,00,000
8.	Limestone	Vempalli belt, Mutsukota, Karnapudi Chinnekkalur	60,000
9.	Steatite (talc)	Mutsukota Tabjaia Karnapudi	1.5 Million
10.	Corundum	Konampalle– Parigi Sector	1.5 Million

Source : Department of Industries, Government of Andhra Pradesh Action Plan—1983–84 to 1989–90, For Industrial Development of Anantapur district, D.I.C., Anantapur p. 9.

crores provision has been under the Annual Action Plan 1987 including the programme of self Employment programme for Educated un-Employed youth.

The Table 2.5 furnish the details of financial institutional that are serving the Anantapur District.

Table 2.5 : The Institution-wise Network of Branches in the District as on 31-03-1988

S.No.	*Group*	*Name of the Bank*	*No. of Branches*
1.	State Bank Group	State Bank of India	29
		State Bank of Hyderabad	1
		State Bank of Mysore	1
2.	Nationalised Banks	Andhra Bank	20
		Canara Bank	7
		Corporation Bank	6
		Indian Bank	1
		Syndicate Bank	27
		Union Bank of India	1
		Vijaya Bank	2
3.	Private Sector Banks	Karnataka Bank Ltd.,	4
		Karuru Vysya Bank Ltd.,	1
		The Vysya Bank Ltd.,	2
4.	Regional Rural Bank	Sree Anantha Grameena Bank	67
5.	Co-operative Banks	The Anantapur District Co-operative Bank Ltd.	13
		Co-operative Agricultural Development Bank Ltd.,	10
6.	Other Financing Institutions	A.P. State Finance Corporation	1
		Total	**202**

Source : Department of Industries, *Government of Andhra Pradesh, 'Action Plan—1983-84 to 1989-90* for Industrial Development of Anantapur District, DIC., Anantapur p. 15

Industrial Development

The industrial development is concentrated mostly in urban areas. The industrial sector in the district is not developed sufficiently to absorb the increasing number of unemployed youth both unskilled and educated.

The district has 3,177 grounded factories employing

34,287 (approx.) workers. The district Industries Centres has been functioning from 1978. There are four Industrial Estates at Anantapur, Tadapatri, Kadiri and Hindupur and Industrial Development area at Guntakal. An Industrial Development area has been recently established at Thumukunta (Hindupur) with an extent of 399 acres. Plots have been developed and are available for allotment to the prospective industrialists. Another Industrial Estate is under development at Gooty.

The Table 2.6 analyses the position of existing Industrial Estates and industrial Development areas.

Table 2.6 : Existing Industrial Estates/ Industrial Development Areas

Sl. No.	*Particulars*	*I*	*II*	*III*	*IV*	
					Plots	*Sheds*
1.	Assisted Private Industrial Estate, Anantapur	59.05	72	..	..	..
2.	Rural Industrial Estate, S. Sadla Palli, Hindupur	38.13	39	10	2	..
3.	Industrial Estate, Kadiri	49.29	61	8	15	..
4.	Industrial Estate, Tadipatri	9.09	13	8	..	3
5.	Industrial Development Area, Guntakal	57.81	36	4	9	..
6.	Industrial Development Area, Thumakunta, Hindupur	395.78	236	12	190	12
7.	Industrial Estate, Gooty	51.62	Under-development	Under construction	..	..

Note : I –Extend of Land Developed (acres);
II –Number of Plots developed;
III –Number of sheds constructed;
IV –Vacancy available for allotment (on 01-02-'89).

Source : District Indusries Centre, Anantapur.

Small-Scale Industries

3,156 Small Scale Industries are established in the district with a capital investment of Rs. 24,29 crores providing employment to 21,211 persons. It is proposed to set up 2,000 small units during the VII plan period. The Table 2.7 and 2.8 indicate the position of enterprises and industries on 31.03.1989 of Anantapur district respectively.

Table 2.7 : Position of Enterprises in the District as on 31-03-89

1.	Small Scale Industries	3156
	Investment in Lakhs	2153.43
	Employment	21211
	Financial Assistance in Lakhs	2429.39
2.	Self Employment Scheme	1754
	Investment in Lakhs	301.87
	Employment	1754
3.	Artisan Complexes	34
	Investment in Lakhs	113.55
	Beneficiaries	972
4.	Artisan Clusters	52
	Investment in Lakhs	48.41
	Beneficiaries	1072
5.	Industrial Co-operatives	41
	Members	2446
	Paid-up Share Capital in Lakhs	1.67
	Working Capital in Lakhs	9.86

Source : District Industries Centre, Anantapur.

Incentives and Concessions

A package of incentives for setting up industries is available is Andhra Pradesh right from 1969 onwards.

Anantapur is now one of the three districts selected by the State Government and one among twelve districts in the country chosen by Government of India for intensive industrial development declaring it as an Intensive Industrial Development Area with new and additional package of incen-

Table 2.8 : Large and Medium-Scale Industries in Anantapur District

Sl. No.	*Name*	*Activity*	*Investment (in lakhs)*	*Employment*
1.	Super Spinning Mills	Cotton Yarn	774.00	1372
2.	Premier Cotton Mills	Cotton Yarn	452.00	370
3.	Super Spinning Mills	Cotton Yarn	412.00	528
4.	Andhra Co-op. Spng.Mills	Cotton Yarn	193.00	1809
5.	ATP Cotton Mills	Cotton Yarn	111.00	453
6.	ATP. Mulbury Silks	Silk FABS	146.50	115
7.	RPGT Yarn Processing	Yarn Processing	70.40	60
8.	MG. Mettalic Springs	INDL. Springs	37.00	93
9.	HYD. Allwyn Ltd.	Watch Assembly	13.24	119
10.	Pattabhi Forge Ltd.	Forgings	100.00	100
11.	AP. Lightings Ltd.	GLS Lamps	107.00	252
12.	Nizam Sugars Ltd.	Sugar	361.00	425
13.	Markfed	G.N. Oil	40.00	74
14.	Kalyan Flour Mills	Wheat Products	54.00	34
15.	Madhu Oil Refinery	Refined Oil	63.00	74
16.	Polytec. Organics	Liquid Glucose	189.00	137
17.	Nandi Pipes Pvt. Ltd.	PVC Pipes	185.00	100
18.	ELGI Tyre Treads	Tyre Treads	230.00	106
19.	Dadha Bros. Ltd.	RECL. Rubber	101.00	49
20.	Shanti Castings	Alloy Casting	105.00	62
21.	Bharat Gold Mines	Gold	395.00	500
		Total	4139.14	6832

Source : District Industries Centre, Anantapur.

tives in addition to the Central Incentives available for whole of the district.

The details of Central and new package of State Incentives available for new Industries are given below:

Central Incentives

1) Central capital investment subsidy at 15 per cent subject to a ceiling of Rs. 15 lakhs for all new industrial units

coming up in (former Panchayat Samithi) 1. Singanamala, 2. Tadipatri, 3. Gooty and 4. Kudair blocks.

2) Central capital investment subsidy at 10 per cent to a ceiling of Rs. 10 lakhs is available to all new Industrial Units coming up in (former Panchayat Samithi) 1. Hindpur, 2. Madakasira, 3. Dharmavaram, 4. Penukonda, 5. Rayadurg. 6. Kanekal, 7. Kambadur, 8. Uravakonda, 9. Kalyandurg, 10. Chinakothakota, 11. Kadiri East and 12. Kadiri West Blocks.

3) In addition the following concessions are offered by the financial institutions and the Government of India.

   i) Taxable income of new industrial undertakings get exempted upto 20 per cent for a period of 10 years.

   ii) Shares subscribed for new industries are exempted from wealth tax for a period of 5 years.

   iii) Upto Rs. 3,000/- of dividend income is exempted from Income Tax.

   iv) Term loans of concessional rate of interest which generally 2 to 2.5 per cent than normal rates.

   v) N.R.D.C. Financing upto 5 per cent of the expenditure of the project for development work.

   vi) Lesser contribution of promoters.

   vii) Lesser commitment charges.

   viii) Longer repayment period from 10 to 20 years.

   ix) Moratorium on repayment of loans upto 5 years.

   x) Preferred import facilities both for capital equipment and raw materials.

New Package of State Incentives

A. Any large industry with an investment of Rs. 10 crores

and above offering an employment of 250 persons would be entitled to the following incentives;

1) Land

Suitable dry land required for the industry upto 50 acres for each industry would be identified from government lands and given free of cost after assessing the required land in the proportion of free space to built-up areas. In the ratio 1:6. If the Government land is not available, the industries would be assisted in acquiring private dry lands as per Land Acquisition Act and the cost subsidised to the extent of the appraised requirement of land and at rate not exceeding Rs. 5,000/- per acre.

2) Investment Subsidy

The industry would be entitled to an investment subsidy of 15 per cent on the fixed capital investment on land, building and machinery subject to a ceiling of Rs. 15 Lakhs. This will include any Central Investment Subsidy payable to the Industry.

3) Power

At present, the Andhra Pradesh State Electricity Board offers 25 per cent tariff concession for the first three years for certain industries. This concession would be extended to two more years i.e., a total of 5 years. Twenty-five per cent concession tariff would be met for the additional 2 years out of the Industrial budget.

4) Water

For the first five years, only 75 per cent of the economic cost of providing water would be charged water is drawn from a public source and provided by the Government.

5) Sales

a) The Sales Tax payable by the industry for the first years commencing from the date of commercial production would be allowed on deferred payments basis up to a maximum of Rs. 1.0 crore or 15 percent of the total value of the fixed assets of the unit whichever is lower subject to the condition that the amount of sales tax deferred during any particular year shall not exceed Rs. 30 Lakhs.

The total amount of sales tax deferred would become payable without interest from the commencement of sixth year from the date of Commercial production in five equal annual instalments.

b) Other Industries (i.e. Industries not fulfilling investment and employment criteria mentioned for item A above) set up in the Industrial Development Areas:

1) **Investment Subsidy** : The industry would be entitled to an investment subsidy of 15 per cent of the fixed capital investment on land, building and machinery subject to a ceiling of Rs. 15.00 lakhs. This will include any Central Investment Subsidy payable to the industry.

2) **Power** : At present, the Andhra Pradesh State Electricity Boards offers 25 per cent tariff concession for the first 3 years for certain industries. This concession would be extended to two more years i.e. a total 5 years. 25 per cent concession tariff would be met for the additional 2 years from out of the Industries Budget.

3) **Water** : For the first 5 years, only 75 per cent of the economic cost of providing water would be charged wherever water is drawn from a public source and provided by the Government.

4) **Sales Tax** : The Sales Tax payable by the industry for the first five years commencing from the date of commercial production would be allowed on deferred payment basis upto a maximum of Rs. 50.00 lakhs or 15 per cent of the total value of the

fixed assets of the unit whichever is lower subject to the condition that the amount of sales tax deferred during any particular year shall not exceed Rs. 20.00 lakhs.

The total amount of sales tax deferred would become payable without interest from the commencement of sixty year from the date of commercial production in five equal annual instalments.

The new package component of State Incentives is available to all Industrial Units, except 65 categories of common placed industries which commenced regular production on or ater 1.4.1984 including substantial expansions, modernisation and diversification.

Notes :

1. Chief Planning Officer, "*Hand Book of Statistics—Anantapur District*", 1983–84, Anantapur, p.1.
2. *Ibid.*, p. 1.
3. Bureau of Economics and Statistics, Government of Andhra Pradesh, "*Statistical Abstract of Andhra Pradesh*", 1981.
4. Bureau of Economics and Statistics, Government of Andhra Pradesh, "*District Profile (Population and General Features) of Anantapur District*", based on 1981 census, Hyderabad.
5. Government of Andhra Pradesh, "*Fifth Five Year Plan of Andhra Pradesh*", Hyderabad, 1973, p. 605.
6. Government of Andhra Pradesh, "Seventh Five Year Plan", Vol. I, Hyderabad, p. 8.
7. Government of Andhra Pradesh, "*Andhra Pradesh District Gazetters*", Anantapur (Revised Edition), Hyderabad, 1970, p. 317.

3

Financial Assistance of APSFC to Small-Scale Industries

Andhra Pradesh State Financial Corporation (APSFC)

Genesis

The Andhra Pradesh State Financial Corporation (APSFC) is a State level Development Bank established under the State Financial Corporation's Act, 1951 (Central Act 63 of 1951) on the 1st November, 1956 with the amalgamation of the erst-while State Financial Corporation of Hyderabad and Andhra States to give impetus to industrial development of the State by providing medium and long term finances to the eligible industrial units in the State[1]. The Corporation has completed 34 years of commendable services for the cause of industrialisation in the State of Andhra Pradesh. At present the Corporation with its head quarters at Hyderabad has been rendering services through the branches and field offices. Each branch has allotted its own jurisdiction covering specified areas.

Internal Organisation

A series of measures have been taken, since inception

to strengthen and streamline the organisation. The Corporation continues to pursue its operations through its existing net work of 20 Branches and four field offices. The Corporation is thinking in terms of opening more full fledged branches when necessity arises.

To cope with the anticipated increase of operations and work load thereon, the Corporation has finalised the recruitments in different cadres from sub-staff level to deputy managers. The Corporation has recruited certain financial and technical officers altogether 31, 8 Assistants, 16 sub-Staff during the year 1988-89, under review the total staff strength including deputationists as on 31st March, was 718 as against 676 at the end of the previous year. The Corporation has one administrative cell to look after the man-power planning and development, personnel administration and other general administrative matters. The Corporation has also one-internal audit cell to audit the accounts of Head Office and also the branches. The Corporation has a monitoring cell to monitor and for the implementation of schemes of the assisted units on schedule and for the revival of the sick units.

A review of the present organisational setup including working of branches is being made in the light of the previous experience and suitable changes in placement of staff, allocation of duties etc., are being considered by the Corporation. In response to the growing demand of the Corporation and as a measure of a career development, promotions were permitted up to the rank of deputy managers on basis of merit. This new system of merit promotions is expected to have an impact on efficiency of the organisation in the long run. Further the requirement of additional staff is being reviewed and necessary steps are being taken to strengthen the organisation at various levels with the expansion of the branches and by improving the operations of the Corporation.

Training Personnel

The Corporation has been laying greater emphasis in

the training of the its officers and staff, while all the new recruits to Corporation are given induction, orientation training. Because the Corporation is conscious of the vital role played by the human resources is achieving its objectives and goals. The training and management development activity has been identified as one of the mechanisms of developing human resources. Thus the Corporation is deputing its employees to various external training programmes.

The Corporation deputed 108 of its officers and staff members to various programmes, seminars, workshops etc., conducted by Administrative Staff College of India, institute of Public Enterprise, Industrial Development Bank of India Training Centre, Management Development Institute, National Institute of Training and Industrial Engineering, National Institute of Small Industry Extension and Training. Bankers Training College, RBI Bombay, Institute of Public Administration, Hyderabad, National Productivity Council. Institute of Financial Management Research, Madras etc.

Management

The overall guidance and policy framing of the Corporation is vested with a Board of Directors comprising and Managing Director appointed by the State Government in consultation with IDBI and eleven directors. Out of them the chairman and three other directors are nominated by the State Government, two directors are nominated by the IDBI and one director is nominated by RBI and one each is elected by Scheduled Commercial Banks, Insurance Companies, Cooperative institutions and individual share holders. Besides the Board of Directors, there is also an executive committee consisting of 6 members, including the Managing Director. The day-to-day administration of the Corporation is left in the hands of managing directors and the general manager.

Objectives

The objectives of the State Financial Corporation are to meet the medium and long term credit requirements of small and medium-scale industries irrespective of the nature of the organisation of the industrial concern. The objective of APSFC, in particular, is to meet the unfulfilled term credit needs of the medium and small-scale industrial concerns located in the State of Andhra Pradesh.

The APSFC is empowered to transact the following kinds of business and its financial assistance can be in any of the following forms, viz.,

1) Guaranteeing loans raised by industrial concerns from scheduled Banks or State Co-operative Bank for a period for exceeding 20 years;
2) Guaranteeing deferred payments due from any industrial concern with the purchase of capital goods
3) Underwriting of the issue of shares and bonds by industrial concern
4) Subscribing to the shares of debentures of industrial concerns
5) Granting loans or advances and subscribing to debentures of an industrial concern repayable within a period not exceeding 20 years from the date of which there are payable
6) Long terms loans to industrial concerns, primarily for the purpose of acquiring fixed assets in the shape of land, building and machinery.
7) Guaranteeing loans raised by industrial concerns which are floated in the public market for a period not exceeding 20 years
8) Acting as an agent of the State or the Central Government or any other financial institutions notified in this behalf by the central Government
9) Foreign exchange loans under IAD line of credit World Bank

10) Loans in collaboration with IDBI, IFCI and ICICI

The Corporation lending policy, in general is governed by market conditions, performance of similar units, policy guidelines of Government and IDBI and statutory provisions. The Corporation provides financial assistance for setting up of new industrial units and also for expansion, diversification or for modernisation of existing ones. Financial assistance on concessional terms is also available for setting-up of new industrial units in notified backward areas.

Any industrial concerns under any form of ownership, whether it be a proprietory or partnership concern, Joint Hindu family, registered co-operative society, private or public limited company engaged in or proposed to engage in one or more of the following activities, are eligible for financial assistance.

a) The manufacture, preservation or processing of goods

b) Mining and development goods of mines

c) The hotel industry

d) The transport of passengers or goods by road or by water or by air or by rope-way

e) The generation and distribution of electricity or any other form of power

f) The maintenance, repair, testing or servicing of machin ery of any description or vehicles or vessels or motor boats or trailers or tractors.

g) Assembling, repairing or packing any article with the aid of machinery of power

h) For setting-up or development of an industrial area/ estate

i) Finishing or providing share facilities for fishing or maintenance thereof

j) The research and development of any or product in respect of industrial activities eligible for assistance by SFC

k) Providing of weight bridge facilities

l) Providing special or technical knowledge or other services for the promotion of industrial growth

m) For setting-up Nursing homes/Hospitals and for medical equipment to Doctors

In the case of proprietary and partnership concerns, the maximum assistance eligible is a Rs. 30 lakhs and in case of limited companies and co-operative societies, the maximum limit has been extended to Rs. 60 lakhs. The Corporation will advance its loans and extent other financial assistance only to industrial concerns having a paid up capital and free reserves not exceeding a limit of Rs. 3 crores. The Corporation does not extent financial assistance towards working capital except under composite loan scheme and single window scheme.

In order to achieve its objectives, the Corporation has been operating following various schemes keeping in view the changing needs of wide range of entrepreneurs to avail financial assistance for establishing industrial ventures.

1) Composite Loan Scheme

The composite loan scheme was introduced during the year 1979-80 in order to help the artisans in rural areas and in urban areas where population is below five lakhs. The novel features of the scheme is that 100 percent cost of the scheme including working capital would be financed by the Corporation. The Scheme was designed primarily to promote village and tiny sector units for the benefit of craftsmen and artisans in the rural areas of the State. The Scheme has been providing employment opportunities to the rural masses and helping reduce regional imbalances. Under this scheme, Corporation is extending financial assistance to establish clusters of units with raw-materials and market tie-up arrangements in co-ordination with other district level promotional agencies wherever possible. Under this scheme, the loan assistance is up to Rs. 50,000 for promotion of industries in cottage, village and tiny sector.Loan against the working capital shall also be considered, moratorium period under the scheme should be 12-18 months. Repayment period is from 3 to 10 years. Further thrust has been given to his scheme during 1987-88 by reduction of interest by 1 percent and also specific targets were assigned to branch offices for sanctioning assistance under the scheme.

During 1988-89, the Corporation provided assistance to 1087 entrepreneurs and the sanctioned amount was Rs. 4.13 crores as against Rs. 3.7 crores to 1032 units in 1987-88. The cumulative effective sanctions and disbursements as on 31st March, 1989 were Rs. 10.90 crores and Rs. 5.14 crores respectively. An analysis of the trend in sanctions of composite loans shows that out of the cumulative effective amount sanctioned under this scheme, more than 35 percent have taken place in the financial year 1988-89.

2) Special Capital Assistance

The Corporation has been operating the special capital and the seed capital scheme to provide soft loan assistance to bridge the gap in equity of upcoming first generation entrepreneurs who do not have adequate financial resources but have viable project ideas. This soft loan is provided at 1 per cent per annum interest service charge, repayment of which commences 3 to 5 years after the initial moratorium for repayment of principal amount 20% of the project cost or Rs. 4 lakhs whichever is less to bridge the gap in minimum promoter's contribution is extended. In order to expedite sanctions and disbursement of special capital loans to Scheduled Caste entrepreneurs, power of sanction and disbursements of special capital loans to Scheduled Caste entrepreneurs have been delegated to the branch manager in the year 1988 under review. During 1988-89 the Corporation sanctioned soft loans to 262 entrepreneurs amounting to Rs. 200.98 lakhs and disbursed an amount of Rs. 203.22 lakhs. The cumulative effective sanctions under this scheme were Rs. 1125 lakhs to 1524 entrepreneurs. The cumulative disbursement at the end of March, 1984 under this scheme was Rs. 859.66 lakhs.

3) IDBI Seed Capital Assistance

The Corporation has been operating the IDBI seed capital scheme for the financial year 1983-84 in respect of small scale units as on agency function. This scheme is similar to special capital assistance scheme. Under this scheme, Industrial units being set-up by new technocrat entrepreneurs or craftsmen i.e., artisans or other persons who may not have academic qualification, but possess some practical experience or skill in the line, are eligible to an extent of 20 per cent of project cost to a maximum of Rs. 1 lakh to bridge the gap in minimum promoter's contribution. Repayments offer intial moratorium period of maximum 5 years. Under this scheme, soft loan assistance is provided in excess of Rs. 4 lakhs available under special capital assistance. The in-house screening committee comprising the nominees of IDBI as well as SFC recommends to IDBI for sanction of seed capital assistance of over Rs. 4 lakhs and upto 5 lakhs. The proposals in excess of Rs. 5 lakhs are referred to the main screening committee of IDBI for sanction of seed capital assistance. During 1988-89 three units were sanctioned assistance under seed capital scheme involving an amount of Rs. 13.50 lakhs and disbursed an amount of Rs. 77 lakhs. Cumulative sanctions and disbursements at the end of march, 1989 under this scheme were Rs. 428 lakhs and Rs. 369 lakhs respectively.

4) Transport Loans Scheme

In order to facilitate movement of inputs to the industries as well as manufacture items from the units, importance continues to be given to assistance to transport sector, except in the cases of Hyderabad and Rangareddy districts. The Corporation has taken a policy decision to finance light commercial vehicle (LCVs). The transport loans schemes are in operation in five selected districts where the transport with ESCOM tie-up. The districtwise quotas were fixed based on recovery performance in this portfolio. Under this scheme, the financial assistance considered for acquiring 1 to 6 vehicles to single road transport operators (SRTO) for transportation of goods with 50 percent collateral security. For SC/ST/ Ex-Servicemen entrepreneurs only 25 percent collateral security will be given. during 1988-89 the Corporation sanctioned to the transport sector was R.s 1794.35 lakhs to 845 entrepreneurs as against Rs. 16.47 crores to 740 entrepreneurs during the previous year. The cumulative effective assistance sanctioned to the transport sector was Rs. 9830.67 lakhs to 5216 entrepreneurs whereas disbursements and outstanding made under the scheme were Rs. 8560.85 lakhs and Rs. 2851.62 lakhs respectively as at 31st march, 1989.

5) Scheme of Assistance to Physically Handicapped and SC/ST Entrepreneurs

In order to help the physically handicapped in taking up self-employment by entering to the field of entrepreneurship, the Corporation operates this scheme by providing 100 per cent financial assistance for equipment of working capital or both. Maximum amount of loan should not exceed Rs. 50.00. During the current financial year an amount of Rs. 13.99 lakhs to 18 entrepreneurs was sanctioned and an amount of 9.91 lakhs was disbursed.

The Corporation is committed to develop sound entrepreneurial base among weaker sections of society in general and scheduled castes in particular during VIIth plan period. During the year 1987-88 under review, the Corporation intensified its efforts in identifying the potential scheduled caste entrepreneurs in liaison with other district level agencies to extent liberal assistance them. The Branch offices were assigned specific target to sanction loans to SC/ST. entrepreneurs under various schemes operated by the Corporation. The branch officials have attended industrial compaigns conducted in various districts and identified SC/ST entrepreneurs for providing assistance. In order to help the scheduled castes and scheduled tribes to enter the field of entrepreneurship, a special scheme also is being operated by the Corporation. For projects with the cost exceeding Rs. 50,000 financial assistance shall be extended on liberal terms including soft loan assistance to SC/ST entrepreneurs. During 1988-89 special interest has been given to extend term loans to (including soft loans) SC entrepreneurs ws Rs. 841.30 lakhs to 690 applications whereas the amount sanctioned to Scheduled Tribe entrepreneur was Rs. 130.70 lakhs to 82 applications which includes soft loan. Under this scheme SC/ST entrepreneurs have been provided soft loan assistance at nominal service charges of 1 percent to meet the short fall in their margin money recruitments. An amount of Rs. 103.46 lakhs (gross) was sanctioned to 182 Scheduled Caste entrepreneurs as soft loans and Rs. 17.62 lakhs to 23 Scheduled Tribes entrepreneurs.

6) Self Employment for the Ex-Servicemen (SEMFEX)

Rehabilitation of ex-servicemen (as well as their widows), who have dedicated their lives for as preservation of the freedom of our country, is the social responsibility of one and all. In order to fulfil this objective, the Corporation has started operating this scheme in association with Director-General of Resettlement. Under this scheme, assistance is provided to ex-servicemen as well as widows of the ex-servicemen, and disabled service personnel for starting small-scale industries and operating transport vehicles at concessional rate of interest and at reduced margins. Under this scheme the cost of project should be within Rs. 12.00 lakhs. Soft loan assistance up to 15 percent. Repayment is permitted over a period of 10 years with 1-2 years of moratorium. No security is required under the scheme except for transport vehicle.

During 1988-89 the Corporation sanctioned Rs. 176.69 lakhs under this scheme which included soft loans provided to and disbursed Rs. 102.24 lakhs.

7) Women Entrepreneurs Schemes

The Corporation introduced women Entrepreneurs Scheme with the effect from 1.5.1987 to encourage women entrepreneurs to set-up industrial ventures in the small-scale sector. Special development programmes were conducted at various places in the districts by the industrial promotional agencies in which the Corporation actively participated. Under this scheme, womens' share in equity should be atleast 51 percent and have experience and training in the related field of manufacture. Assistance shall be given at a maximum DET* of 3:1 with a minimum promoters contribution at 15 percent of project cost in Small-Scale Industrial sector. Loan will be repayable over ten years with a moratorium period of two years. During 1988-89 an amount of Rs. 629.5 lakhs was sanctioned to 209 women entrepreneurs as against Rs. 355 lakhs to 226 candidates during the previous year.

8) Single Window Scheme

In order to help the small entrepreneurs to obtain terms finance as well as working capital requirements at a single, course, the Government of India has formulated single window scheme. The Corporation has brought this scheme into implementation towards the end of this financial year and detailed guidelines were provided to branch offices for implementation of this scheme. Only new tiny and small units with project cost (excluding working capital margin) which does not exceed Rs. 5.00 lakhs and total working capital requirements at the normal level of operation up to Rs. 2.5 lakhs are eligible for assistance under the scheme. The debt equity ratio shall be 3:1 for the total venture outlay (i.e. cost of the project and total working requirements as mentioned above). The Corporation could sanction an amount of Rs. 2.15 lakhs to 7 industrial units under this scheme. This scheme enables an entreneur to receive assistance up to Rs. 5.00 lakhs, the maximum celing for working being 2.5 lakhs.

---

* Debt Equity Ratio.

9) Relief Assistance for Natural Calamities, Riots etc.

The Corporation always rises to the occasion wherever entrepreneurs face problems of dislocation in the functioning of their units, including destruction of assets due to unforeseen condition either due to advance in whether or to any catestrophe. Under this scheme, all units assisted by SFC or self-financed, which are affected by the floods and other natural calamities, are eligible for assistance up to maximum of Rs. 5 lakhs. Mortorium period is 6 to 12 months. There is no commitment charges. During December, 1988 the industrial units in Coastal districts were affected due to riots and in order to help the rehabilitation of these units the Corporation promptly sanctioned loans to the affected units. Assistance provided during 1988-89 under this scheme was Rs. 107.59 lakhs to 37 units. This assistance includes loans sanctioned for lorries, whether burnt fully as partially.

10) Scheme for Rehabiliation Assistance

In order to help the revival of potentially viable sick small and medium scale industries, the Corporation extends assistance at concessional rates of interest.

a) For Sick SSI Units

SSI Units assisted by SFC is eligible for assistance under the scheme. The unit will be classified as sick if it incurred cash losses during the previous accounting year and there is erosion in its net worth to the extent of 50 per cent or more. Rehabilitation loan is for —

- minimum capital expenditure required for restarting/operating the unit.
- margin money for additional working capital needed for rehabilitation start for expenses.

b. For Sick Medium-scale Units

A medium sector industrial concern would be deemed as a 'Sick' industrial concern for the purpose of the scheme provided. An industrial company or a co-operative society has been incorporated/registered for not less than 7 years prior to the date of rehabilitation. In the case of sole proprietary, partnership firms, it shall be five years.

The industrial concern should have accumulated losses equal to or exceeding its entire net worth and should have also suffered cash losses in current financial year and the immediately preceding financial year. Rehabilitation loan is for —

- minimum capital expenditure required for restarting/operating the unit.
- margin money for additional working capital needed for rehabilitation/startup expenses. During 1988-89 the Corporation sanctioned an amount of Rs. 326.57 lakhs to 20 units as against Rs. 334 lakhs to 11 units in the previous year. Disbursements during 1988-89 were Rs. 269.14 lakhs.

11) 100 per cent Export-Oriented Scheme

In order to help the units in promoting exports which, in turn, helps in the inflow of foreign exchange, the Corporation is operating a special scheme. Under the Scheme, all such units are eligible for rebate of 20 per cent on the interest payment made on Rupee loans (not foreign exchange loan component) for the first 5 operating years provided their export sales reach or exceed 25 per cent of the total sales. Export sales of the concern's own manufactured goods will be reckoned at FOB value and the concerns aggregate sales will be net of excise duty. The scheme will be in operation to the end of March, 1990. During the current financial year the Corporation sanctioned Rs. 209.79 lakhs to 10 units and disbursed on amount of Rs. 18.55 lakhs under this scheme.

12) Modernisation Scheme

In order to encourage modernisation of industries with the introduction of modern technology for improvement in productivity, the Corporation is operating this scheme. At least 5 years of operation is required for the unit. Proposals should made a case for the need for modernisation and the benefits that would accrue by way of reduction in unit cost of production, upgradation of technology, higher productivity and better profitability and is not for mere replacement expansion of capacity. Assistance under this scheme is eligible for 1 per cent reduction in the normal rate of interest., During 1988-89 the Corporation sanctioned an amount of Rs. 62.08 lakhs to 14 units under this scheme.

13) Equipment Refinance Scheme (ERS)

Under this scheme, the Corporation extends financial assistance to well-established small and smaller industrial concerns, for acquisition of capital goods/equipments not related to any specific projects both indigenous and for modernisation/expansion and/or for balancing/replacement purpose. Period or repayment shall be two to five years inclusive or moratorium of 6 to 12 months. The unit should have been in operation for at least 4 years, and should have declared profits during the two preceding accounting years. During 1988-89 sanctions under this scheme were Rs. 284.23 lakhs for 47 applicants as against Rs. 86 lakhs to 141 units in 1987-88. Entrepreneurs seeking assistance under this scheme receive assistance in shortest time.

14) Medical Loans

It is the social responsibility of any public institution to help in extending medical facilities to the nook and corner of the State so that people can have access to needy medical assistance. With this objective in view, the Corporation has introduced this scheme under which assistance is provided for acquiring electo-medical equipment by the doctors. Preference will be given to specialist doctors who intend to start clinics in towns and rural areas for providing medical amenities in the area. All doctors who are full time practioners with a minimum of 3 years experience are eligible for the help. For setting-up of hospitals and nursing homes also, the Corporation extends assistance. Under the medical loans schemes, financial assistance is provided for nursing homes/hospitals having a bed strength between 20 and 50. Expansion/modernisation of existing hospitals and nursing homes may also be considered provided that after expansion/modernisastion the beds should be less than 50. The hospital shall have a M.D./M.S. qualified doctor on full time basis. During the year, under review an amount of Rs. 406.32 lakhs to 49 applicants was sanctioned for establishment of nursing homes whereas Rs. 60.24 lakhs to 29 persons were sanctioned for purchase of medical equipment.

15) Scheme for Quality Control Facilities by Small-Scale Industrial Units

In addition to the financial assistance to private agencies/entrepreneurs for developing any area in to an industrial area/estate at potential rural and semi urban areas, the Corporation introducted scheme for quality control facilities by Small-Scale Industrial units for better market acceptability of their products. Second hand machinery cannot be financed under this scheme. Maximum assistance is up to Rs. 7.50 lakhs and moratorium is upto 3 years and repayment will be within 8 years.

16) Assistance for Diesel Generating Sets

Industrial Units continue to suffer from the power cut. In order to ensure continuous power supply to them, the Corporation has been extending assistance for purchase of diesel generating sets. The Corporation has liberalised the policy in this regard. Only when the client is a willful defaulter in repayment of his dues to the Corporation, he will not be sanctioned loans for purchase of Diesel Generating Sets and get over the problem of power cuts. During the current year an amount of Rs. 256.66 lakhs was sanctioned for purchase for 96 diesel sets.

Performance of Andhra Pradesh State Financial Corporation (A.P.S.F.C)

The Andhra Pradesh State Financial Corporation (APSFC) was established on 3.11.1956 with its head quarters at Hyderabad and with a paid up capital Rs. 150 lakhs. Now the paid up share capital has gone upto Rs. 871.25 lakhs (as on 31st march, 1989). Of this, 46.56 per cent held by the Industrial Development Bank of India (IBI) and the remaining 6.88 percent is held by the Scheduled Banks, Insurance Companies, Co-operative Banks and individual shareholders. In additional, it has reserve fund of Rs. 2,557.06 lakhs and other reserves amounting to Rs. 13.50 lakhs the Corporation has also borrowed a sum of Rs. 15,527.50 lakhs through issue of bonds and debentures. The term borrowings of the Corporation as on 31st March, 1989 stood at Rs. 33,519.96 lakhs. The Corporation earned profit to the tune of 309.20 lakhs with property and assets valued at Rs. 45,736.93 lakhs as on 31st March, 1989.

Operation of the Branches

In order to serve the entrepreneurs effectively, nearer to the place of operations, the Corporation has given emphasis to branch expansion programme. Under the branch expansion programme of the Corporation seven new branch offices have been established during 1984-85 taking the total number of branch offices to 20, in addition to five field offices. The presence of either the branch office or field office in each district is found to be very useful especially for tiny and small-scale entrepreneurs since it avoids travelling all the way to Hyderabad and they can obtain sanctions and disbursements of loans to the extent of Rs. 7.50 lakhs at the branch level itself. Further, during 1985-86, the Corporation has taken the policy decision to further decentralize its operations by 4 more branches in the districts of Mahaboobnagar, Vizianagram, Prakasam and Medak districts of the State by upgrading the existing field offices. No additional branches were opened since 1985 though the branch expansion programme of the Corporation has been yielding good results in the areas of sanctions, disbursements and recovering of loans. Now the Corporation operates through 20 branch Offices and 4 field offices apart from the Head Office. The branch and field offices have been contributing significantly to the industrial development of the State by providing services to the rural entrepreneurs at their door steps in establishing village, cottage and small industries. The Table 3.1 reveals the branch-wise classification of effective sanc-

Table 3.1 : Branch-wise Classification of Term Loans (Effective) Sanctioned, Disbursed as on 31st March, 1989

(Amount in Rs.000's)

Sl. No.	*Name of the Branch*	*Effective Sanctions*		*Disbursements Amount*
		No. of Units	*Amount*	
1.	Adilabad	498	100432	84785
2.	Anantapur	2083	432299	298721
3.	Cuddapah	993	205833	158829
4.	Eluru	996	313138	273062
5.	Guntur	1428	331611	291842
6.	Hyderabad	2478	1991668	1394387
7.	Karimnagar	673	147801	113350
8.	Khammam	674	201428	140956
9.	Kurnool	1484	274979	224920
10.	Nalgonda	1051	471837	332568
11.	Nellore	7608	398405	316109
12.	Nizamabad	772	126400	106859
13.	Rajhamundry	1073	302057	216949
14.	Rangareddy-I	570	269241	220877
15.	Rangareddy-II	3397	1409532	1044871
16.	Srikakulam	800	175522	124786
17.	Tirupati	1781	516679	364441
18.	Vijayawada	1499	517144	412675
19.	Vizag	1449	338558	286108
20.	Warangal	782	185809	134892
	Total	**32243**	**8821036**	**6665267**

Source : Reports of APSFC., Hyderabad

tions and disbursements excluding soft loans and bridge loans since inception up to 31st March, 1989.

Assistance of APSFC

As on 31st March, 1989, the Corporation has received 42,937 application for various forms of financial assistance covering an amount of Rs. 1,28,845.87 lakhs of which the Corporation has sanctioned 38,048 applications for a sum of Rs. 1,07,076.53 lakhs. Small-scale industries account for a lion's share with 41,130 applications amounting to Rs. 91,990.97 lakhs. As on 31st March, 1989 total assistance sanctioned to small-scale units stood at Rs. 76,662,35 lakhs covering 36,571 applications which forms 71.59 per cent and 96.11 per cent to the total cumulative sanctioned amount and number of application respectively, leaving out 4,238 applications which were withdrawn and rejected covering an amount of Rs. 13,160.32 lakhs. The number of applications received, sanctioned, pending and withdrawn/rejected since inception to 31st March, 1989 is provided in Table 3.2.

Table 3.2 : Summary of Applications Received, Sanctioned, Pending and Withdrawn/Rejected upto 31st March, 1989, since Inception

(Amount in Rs. 000's)

Sl. No.	*Particulars*	*Small-Scale Units*		*Others*		*Total*	
		No.	*Amt.*	*No.*	*Amt.*	*No.*	*Amt.*
1.	Applications Received	41130	9199097	1807	3685490	42137	12884587
2.	Applications Sanctioned with Applied Amount	36571	7666235	1477	3041418	38048	10707653
3.	Applications Pending	321	216830	42	96778	363	313608
4.	Applications Withdrawal/ Rejected	4238	1316032	288	547294	4526	1863326

Source : Reports of APSFC., Hyderabad.

The Corporation has recorded substantially higher performance in the operational areas, viz., sanctions and disbursements and recoveries. The total gross sanctions accorded by the Corporation including bridge loans, special capital loans during 1988-89 were Rs. 16,957.23 lakhs as compared to Rs. 13,188.01 lakhs in the previous year registering a growth rate of 29 per cent. The disbursement made by the Corporation during the 1988-89 were also higher by Rs. 11,323.56 lakhs, the highest in the Corporation's existence as compared to Rs. 10,248.93 lakhs during the previous year recording an increase of 10.48 per cent. The Corporation recovered an amount of Rs. 84.86 crores during 1988-89 again the highest in the Corporation's history, registering the growth rate in recoveries being 22.75 per cent over the previous year. The cumulative gross sanctions, disbursements and outstanding at the end of 31st March, 1989 stood at Rs. 1,05,777.43 lakhs, Rs. 68,627,17 lakhs and Rs. 51,884.01 lakhs respectively. The particulars of Corporation's sanctions, disbursements and outstandings are furnished in the Table 3.3.

Table 3.3 : Summary of Corporation's Sanctions, Disbursements and Outstanding During 1987–1989 and as on 31st March, 1989

(Amount in Rs.000's)

Sl. No.	*Particulars*	*1987*	*1988*	*1989*	*As on 31st March, 1989*
1.	Sanctions	1353423	1318801	1695723	10577743
2.	Disbursements	810162	1024893	1132356	6862717
3.	Outstanding	3137723	4317295	5227479	5188401
4.	Recoveries (in crores)	59.65	68.84	84.86	NA

Source : Reports of APSFC., Hyderabad.

A birds eye-view of the financial assistance, according to the nature of the assistance sanctioned, is give in Table 3.4.

It is evident from the Table 3.4 that term loans for various schemes of Corporation predominate the entire

Table 3.4 : Financial Assistance According to the Nature of Assistance Sanctioned (Effective) Disbursed and Outstanding as on 31-03-89

(Amt. Rs. in 000's)

Sl. No.	*Description*	*Effective Sanctions*		*Disbursements*	*Outstanding*
		No.	*Amount*	*Amount*	*Amount*
1.	Loans				
	a) Term Loans	32243	8821036	6665267	5101644
	b) Bridge Loans	584	113332	82033	5645
2.	Special Capital Assistance	1524	112500	85966	77857
3.	Under-writings				
	a) Ordinary Shares	25	8750	6512	3005
	b) Debentures	4	3400	3400	250
[illegible]	Guarantees for loans (D.P.G.)	32	21292	19539	–
	Total :	**34412**	**9080310**	**6862717**	**5188401**

Source : Reports of APSFC., Hyderabad

operations of financial assistance to industrial units. The cumulative effective sanctions of the Corporation accounts for an amount of Rs. 88,210.36 lakhs as terms loans to 32,243 units. This is in addition to the sanction of 584 bridge loans with an amount of Rs. 1,133.32 lakhs and special capital assistance to 1,524 applications to the extent of Rs. 1,125 lakhs. Total disbursements made by the Corporation as on 31st, March, 1989 were Rs. 68,627.17 lakhs. Out of these disbursements towards from loans were Rs. 6,6652.67 lakhs, bridge loans Rs. 820.32 lakhs and special capital assistance Rs. 859.66 lakhs.

The Corporation has not underwritten any share or debenture issues of companies and also not received sanction of deferred payment guarantees for the purchase of indigenous machinery. The effective sanctions under underwriting operations as on 31st March, 1989 were 121.50 lakhs covering the share issue of 29 companies. The net oustanding investment in shares and debentures of various companies as on 31st March, 1989 were Rs. 212.92 lakhs covering 32 units. Of these sanctions the Corporation issued guarantees for a sum of Rs. 195.39 lakhs which were fully met by the units.

Total outstanding of term loans as at the end of March, 1989 under review were R. 51,016.44 lakhs which includes principle and interest. Amount outstanding under bridge loans was Rs. 56.45 lakhs.

Performance of Corporation in the Area of Recoveries

The Corporation has been recording substantially higher performance in one of the operational areas, recoveries during the recent past. The modest performance of the Corporation in the area of recoveries has to be viewed against the backdrop of sever drought in some parts of the State, floods in the other parts of the state, paucity of working capital due to the tight credit policy being followed by the commercial banks, attribution to lack of demand, inadequate of supply of essential industrial raw materials and other factors which debiliated the State's economy resulting in a recession on the industrial front. The general dislocation due to elections to local bodies also hampered Corporation's recovery drives. In spite of the advance factors, in absolute terms, the Corporation's arrears portfolio appeared to be alarming. The details of arreas as on 31.03.1989 are furnished in following Tables i.e., Tables 3.5, 3.6, 3.7 nd 3.8.

Table Table 3.5 shows that the arrears pertaining to a period of over 12-24 months and between 24-36 months worked out to Rs. 2,139.08 (27.24%) and Rs. 977.65 lakhs (12.45%) respectively. This indicates the major share of the overdues is blocked up in chronic cases, most of the units being sick.

The particulars of classification of arrears amount wise as on 31.3.1989 are giver in Table 3.6. It can be observed from the table that arrears about Rs. 1,883.70 lakhs (23.98%) and Rs. 1,310.94 lakhs (16.69%) are blocked up with the units to

Table 3.5 : Age-wise Arrears Position as on 31-03-89, Principal and Interest in Arrears

(Amount in Rs.000's)

Sl. No.	Age of Arrears	No. of Projects	Amount in Arrears		Total	%age of toal
			Prin-cipal	Int-erest		
1.	0 – 3 months	1452	33043	28031	61074	7.78
2.	3 – 6 months	632	18658	6705	25363	3.23
3.	6 – 12 months	1173	57468	37953	95421	12.15
4.	12 – 24 months	1554	113427	100481	213908	27.24
5.	24 – 36 months	864	58108	39657	97765	12.44
6.	36 – 48 months	505	47341	33077	80418	10.24
7.	4 – 5 years	412	36958	33019	69977	8.91
8.	5 – 7 years	409	37850	49621	87471	11.14
9.	7 – 10 years	322	15101	19056	34157	4.35
10.	Above 10 years	111	8138	11691	19624	2.52
	Total :		426092	359291	785383	100.00

Source : Reports of APSFC., Hyderabad.

Table 3.6 : Amount-wise Analysis of Arrears as on 31-03-89

(Amount in Rs.'000)

Sl. No.	Amount Sanctioned (in Rs.)	No. of Pro-jects	Princi-pal	Inte-rest	Total	%age of total
1.	Below 1 lakh	3318	45601	36516	84117	10.71
2.	1 lakh to 2 lakhs	1362	62786	53585	116371	14.82
3.	2 lakhs to 5 lakhs	1563	107094	81276	188370	23.98
4.	5 lakhs to 10 lakhs	576	67022	64072	131094	16.69
5.	10 lakhs to 20 lakhs	274	49096	27807	76903	9.79
6.	20 lakhs to 30 lakhs	169	44087	37093	81180	10.34
7.	Above 30 lakhs	172	50406	56942	107348	13.67
	Total	7434	426092	359291	785383	100.00

Source : Reports of APSFC., Hyderabad.

whom loan assistance was sanctioned between Rs. 2. lakhs to Rs. 5 lakhs and between Rs. 5 lakhs to Rs. 10 lakhs.

The figures in the Table 3.7 shows that the total amount of principal and interest overdue on 31.03.1989 was 7,853.83 lakhs in respect of 7,434 projects excluding the amounts due from the unit file cases and textile mills taken over by National Textile Corporation as against Rs. 5,503 in respect of 6,313 units at the end of the previous year. Out of these food manufacturing industries, and chemical and chemical products occupied first and second position respectively and contributed to arrears of Rs. 1,474.48 lakhs and Rs. 1,144.68 lakhs, constituting 18.77% and 14.57% respectively of the total arrears.

The Table 3.8 reveals that in the cases of backward districts*, the arrears of Rs. 1,225.12 lakhs were blocked up with the units located in Medak and in case of other than backward districts**, maximum amout of Rs. 718.50 lakhs (9.15%) is due from the units located in Ranga Reddy District.

Industrial Analysis

The Corporation extends financial assistance for a wide variety of industrial products and services which is detailed in the Table 3.9 (industrywise analysis). The Table depicts that the Corporation continued its accent on the promotion of small-scale and tiny sector industries and the highest priority of the small-scale units in the operational areas sanctions and disbursements offered by the Corporation. From the sanctions and disbursements offered by the Corpo-

---

* 1. Anantapur	2. Chittoor	3. Warangal
4. Cuddapah	5. Karimnagar	6. Khammam
7. Kurnool	8. Mahaboob Nagar + Ranga Reddy II	9. Medak
10. Nalgonda		11. Nellore
12. Nizamabad	13. Prakasam	14. Srikakulam

** 1. Adilabad	2. East Godavari	3. Guntur
4. Hyderabad	5. Krishna	6. Ranga Reddy
7. Visakhapatnam	8. Vizianagaram	9. West Godavari

Table 3.7 : Industry-wise Break Up of Arrears as on 31st March, 1989

(Amount in Rs. '000)

Sl. No.	*Particulars*	*No. of Projects*	*Amount of Principle and arrears and interest in arrears*	*Percentage of total*
1.	Food Products manufacture	1804	147448	18.77
2.	Bevarage Industries	38	3804	0.49
3.	Tobacco Products	8	1442	0.08
4.	Textile (Cotton, Jute and allied)	513	78023	9.93
5.	Wood products and furniture	249	5888	0.75
6.	Paper and paper products	128	23844	3.03
7.	Printing & publishing	397	20022	2.55
8.	Leather products	36	1291	0.16
9.	Rubber products	144	33109	4.21
10.	Chemical and chemical products	410	114468	14.57
11.	Non-Metallic Mineral products	748	72457	9.22
12.	Basic Metal Industries	147	146083	5.87
13.	Metal products except machinery	364	40621	5.17
14.	Machinery except electric machinery	386	17682	2.25
15.	Transport equipment and spare parts of vehicles	19	4797	0.61
16.	Electrical machinery and appliances	81	14168	1.80
17.	Miscellaneous Manufacturing Industry	1091	84828	10.80
18.	Gas Manufacturing Industry	5	5232	0.67
19.	Hotel (Tourism type)	87	21124	2.69
20.	Transport	774	49052	6.38
	Total	**7434**	**785383**	**100.00**

Source : Reports of APSFC., Hyderabad.

Table 3.8 : Distric-wise Break-up of Arrears as on March 31, 1989

(Amount in Rs. '000)

Sl. No.	*District*	No. of Pages	Amount of Principle & Interest in arrears	Percentage of Total
1.	Adilabad	139	6253	0.79
2.	Anantapur	390	15902	2.02
3.	Cuddapah	287	27624	3.52
4.	West Godavari	275	31320	3.99
5.	Guntur	583	50628	6.45
6.	Hyderabad	438	53445	6.80
7.	Medak	580	122512	15.59
8.	Karimnagar	151	17409	1.58
9.	Khammam	180	12231	2.22
10.	Kurnool	336	24446	3.11
11.	Nalgonda	282	33975	4.32
12.	Nellore	138	11063	1.41
13.	Prakasam	153	21232	2.69
14.	Nizamabad	234	15770	2.01
15.	East Godavari	216	37064	4.72
16.	Ranga Reddy I	431	71850	9.15
17.	Mahaboob Nagar	267	23795	3.05
18.	Ranga Reddy II	559	54939	6.99
19.	Srikakulam	139	6794	0.86
20.	Chittor	549	47210	6.01
21.	Krishna	389	34884	4.44
22.	Visakhapatnam	346	37644	4.79
23.	Vizianagaram	134	11381	1.44
24.	Warangal	238	16112	2.05
	Total	**7434**	**785383**	**100.00**

Source : Reports of APSFC., Hyderabad.

Table 3.9 : Industry-wise Classification of Term Loans sanctioned (Effective) and Disbursed as on 31-03-1989

(Amount in Rs. '000)

S.No.	Type of Industry	Sanctions				Disbursements
		Small-Scale Units		Total Units		Small Scale Industries
		No.	Amount	No.	Amount	Amount
1.	Food Products	4786	965489	4890	1150918	826548
2.	Beverage & Tobacco Products	239	41073	299	132938	48189
3.	Textiles	1529	217260	1677	511548	197012
4.	Wood Products	1007	70941	1009	74701	47373
5.	Paper & paper products	369	107109	405	182360	102827
6.	Printing & Publishing	992	155054	1024	203711	150082
7.	Leather Products	145	72244	154	112295	51440
8.	Rubber Products	272	114071	296	206705	109220
9.	Chemical Products	1677	1042407	1967	1659040	689708
10.	Non-metallic Mineral Products	2501	577145	2582	834875	433745
11.	Transport Vehicles equipment	156	44495	171	79151	40272
12.	Petroleum Products	17	6875	17	6875	6395
13.	Basic Metal Industry	379	185881	454	362783	142880
14.	Metal Products except Machinery and Transport Equipment	705	193542	742	275562	142190

(Contd.)

Table 3.9 : (Contd.)

(Amount in Rs. '000)

S.No.	*Type of Industry*	*Sanctions*				*Disbursements*
		Small-Scale Units		*Total Units*		*Small-Scale Industries*
		No.	*Amount*	*No.*	*Amount*	*Amount*
15.	Machinery except electrical Machinery	1680	334267	1759	524679	302156
16.	Electrical Machinery and appliances	553	221046	623	402227	176668
17.	Misc. manufacture industry	1846	271423	1871	315515	245105
18.	Gas Manufacture (industrial and domestic)	24	13557	40	50051	12450
19.	Medical loans	68	28300	127	89398	10740
20.	Fisheries loans	6392	2789	6392	2789	2789
21.	Electricity generation & supplies	5	1138	5	1138	3634
22.	Hotels	138	200554	311	456717	85987
23.	Road Transport	5216	983967	5216	983967	855085
24.	Other services	26	48646	31	62000	12020
25.	Other Industries	171	71832	181	139093	59230
	Total	**30893**	**5971105**	**32243**	**8821036**	**4780588**

Source : Reports of A.P.S.F.C., Hyderabad.

ration. From the sanctions made since inception to the end of the March, 1989, it is seen that an amount Rs. 88,210.36 lakhs has been sanctioned (effective) to 32,243 industrial units. Out of these, small-scale industries constituted 95.18% of total sanctions in number and 67.69 per cent of total amount sanctioned. The industry wise analysis of loan assistance sanctioned by Corporation to small-scale units also reveals that chemical products occupies the first position with an amount Rs. 10,424.07 lakhs, constituting 17.45 per cent of the total sanctions of Small-Scale Industries, Chemical industry is followed by Transport sector with Rs. 9,839.67 lakhs (16.47%) of sanctions, food processing industry with Rs. 9,654.89 lakhs (16.16%) of sanctions Non-metallic Mineral products with Rs. 5,77,145 lakhs (9.67%). Electricity generation and supplies occupies the last place with an amount of Rs. 11.38 lakhs (6.02%). In terms of disbursements, Road transport sector accounts for the highest with an amount Rs. 8,560.85 lakhs constituting 17.91 percent of total to small-scale units. Food products secured second place with an disbursed amount Rs. 8,265.48 lakhs (17.28%) followed by chemical industrial accounting for 6,879.08 (14.43%) and non-metallic mineral products its share being (4,337.45 lakhs) 9.07%.

It has been the policy of Government to achieve balanced developed of all regions. In accordance with policy of the Government, the Corporation has been laying special emphasis on extending assistance to industrial units in the backward areas like Telengana and Rayalaseema. In this regard, for the speedy development of economically backward areas of the state, the Corporation has been providing number of incentives including concessions in interest rate and margins etc. As a result, small-scale industries have been receiving high priority in the backward districts. The industries promoted in backward districts of the State are provided with a package of incentives by the Corporation, Supplementing the incentives provided by the Government for accelerating economic development of backward districts. The package includes reduction in interest rate, reduction in promoters margin etc. In this regard there has been an overall improvement in the sanctions as well as disbursements to all the regions in general, in backward districts in particular. The region wise analysis of loans sanctioned as well as disbursed and assistance to certainly backward districts are furnished in the Table 3.10.

The Table 3.10 reveals that Telengana region has received the highest amount of effective sanctions Rs. 49,041.48 lakhs consistituting 55.61% of the total loans sanctioned, of these contribution of Small-Scale Industrial is 65.64%. The disbursements of this region is Rs. 35,735.45 lakhs constituting 53.62% of total disbursements of state (Rs. 66,652.67 lakhs). Contribution of Small-Scale Industrial accounts for 69.64% of total disbursements of region. This was followed by the coastal Andhra Region with sanctions and disbursements for an amount of Rs. 24,870.98 (28.19%) Rs. 20,448.1 lakhs (30.67%) respectively and Rayalaseema region with Rs. 14,297.90 lakhs, of sanctions constituting 16.20% and with this 10,469.11 lakhs of disbursements constituting 15.71.

The Table 3.10 also reveals that the Corporation sanctioned an amount of Rs. 31,462.84 lakhs to 20,275 to be located in centrally backward districts. This constitute 96.90% of term loans sanctioned in number and 63.55% of amount sanctioned to small scale units as on 31st March, 1989. Disbursements to small scale units in backward districts account for an amount Rs. 24,947.83 lakhs constituting 69.66% of total disbursements (Rs. 35,81,167 lakhs).

The Table 3.11 analyses the district-wise classification of assistance of Corporation since inception upto 31st March, 1989. From the Table 3.11 it is evident that among all the districts in the State, Medak, Ranga Reddy and Chittoor districts continue to account for a major share in a sanctions and disbursements and also outstanding. It is matter of satisfaction for the Corporation that Medak, Chittoor and Anantapur backward districts occupy first, third and fourth position in the amount sanctioned and disbursed on 31st

Table 3.10 : Region-wise Classification of Assistance Sanctioned (Effective) Disbursed and Assistance to Central Backward Districts as on 31-03-1989

(*Amount in Rs. '000*)

S.No.	*Region*	*Sanctions*				*Disbursements*	
		Small Scale Industries		*All Units*		*Small-Scale Industries*	*All Units*
		No.	*Amount*	*No.*	*Amount*	*Amount*	
1.	Costal Andhra	14586 (47.21)	1751523 (29.33)	15007 (46.54)	2487098 (28.19)	1509948 (31.58)	2044811 (30.67)
2.	Rayalaseema	6164 (19.95)	1005026 (16.83)	6341 (19.66)	1429790 (16.20)	781973 (16.35)	1046911 (15.71)
3.	Telangana	10143 (32.84)	3214556 (53.84)	10895 (33.80)	4904148 (55.61)	2488667 (52.07)	3573545 (53.62)
	Total	30893 (100)	5971105 (100)	32243 (100)	8821036 (100)	4780588 (100)	6665267 (100)
	Assistance to Central Backward Districts	20275	3146284	20922	4950164	2494783	3581167

Source : Reports of A.P.S.F.C., Hyderabad.

Table 3.11 : District-wise Classification of Term Loans (Effective) Sanctions and Disbursements as on 31-03-1989

(Amount in Rs. '000)

S.No.	Name of the Distt.	Sanctions (Effective)				Disbursements	
		Small-Scale Units		Total Units		Small-Scale Units	All Units
		No.	Amount	No.	Amount	Amount	
1.	Adilabad	487	80771	498	100432	67670	84785
2.	Anantapur	2044	307341	2083	432299	224652	298721
3.	Chittoor	1702	312230	1781	516679	239993	364441
4.	Cuddapah	967	156313	993	205833	129799	158824
5.	East Godavari	1015	205155	1073	302057	189122	256149
6.	Guntur	1383	251518	1428	331611	231800	291842
7.	Hyderabad	770	244414	917	447737	200634	350458
8.	Karimnagar	660	130386	673	147801	104116	113350
9.	Khammam	652	150990	674	201428	119821	140956
10.	Krishna	1420	42894	1499	517144	333548	412675
11.	Kurnool	1451	229142	1484	274979	187529	224920
12.	Mahaboobnagar	523	153211	570	269241	126412	220877

Contd.

Table 3.11 : District-wise Classification of Term Loans (Effective) Sanctions and Disbursements as on 31-03-1989.

(Amount in Rs. '000)

S.No.	Name of the Distt.	Sanctions (Effective)				Disbursements	
		Small-Scale Units		Total Units		Small-Scale Units	All Units
		No.	Amount	No.	Amount	Amount	
13.	Medak	1324	795239	1561	1543931	604634	1043929
14.	Nalgonda	991	266166	1051	471837	220554	332568
15.	Nellore	4927	134945	4959	219266	119331	169676
16.	Nizamabad	761	106048	772	126400	91770	106859
17.	Prakasam	2721	140962	2739	179139	118790	146433
18.	Ranga Reddy	3206	1139159	3397	1409532	840740	1044871
19.	Srikakulam	783	115139	800	175522	95066	124716
20.	Vijayanagaram	340	74618	364	110663	55111	284150
21.	Visakhapatnam	1076	229498	1149	338558	192982	286108
22.	Warangal	763	148172	782	185809	112316	134892
23.	West Godavari	921	196794	996	313138	174198	273062
	Total	30893	5971105	32243	8821036	4780588	6665267

Source : Reports of A.P.S.F.C., Hyderabad.

March, 1989. Medak accounted for 17.50 per cent of total amount sanctioned (effective) and 15.66 per cent of amount disbursed. Among the forward districts, Ranga Reddy district continues to receive substantial amount in terms of total amount of sanctions and disbursements. The districts share in total amount sanctioned was 15.97 per cent and disbursed 15.65 percent respectively. In terms of numbers of loans Nellore district stands first (4,954 units) as on 31st March, 1989.

Small-Scale industries continue to receive the highest priority in the assistance offered by the corporation. As on 31st March, 1989 the Corporation sanctioned (effective) on amount of 59,711.05 lakhs to 30,893 units., and disbursed an amount of Rs. 47,805.88 lakhs. This constitutes 67.69% of total amount sanctioned and 95.81% of total sanctions in number and 71.72% of amount disbursed. Regarding to small-scale units, Ranga Reddy, Medak, Krishna occupy the first, second, third position with the sanctioned amount of Rs. 11,391.59 lakhs, 7,952,39 lakhs and Rs. 4,028.94 lakhs respectively. Karimnagar district enjoys the major individual share with 88.21% of districts sanctions and 91.85% of districts' disbursements.

It can be observed from the table 3.12 that in terms of the number of loans sanctioned upto 10,000 top the list with 8,041 sanctions, followed by loans sanctioned in the range of Rs. 1,00,001 to 2,00,000 numbering 6,752. But in terms of the total amount of loans sanctioned loans in the range of Rs. 2,00,001 to 5,00,000 tops the list with an amount of Rs. 20,31,230 followed by loans in the range of Rs, 20,00,001 to 30,00,001 amounting to Rs. 20,03,080 and loans in the range of Rs, 10,00,001 to 20,00,000 amounting to Rs, 13,97 1.36 lakhs.

The individual particulars of the sanctions, amount disbursed and amount outstanding from the various types of small-scale units, viz public limited companies, private limited companies, co-operatives partnership concerns, joint Hindu family concerns, proprietary concerns and other societies are furnished in the Table 3.13.

Table 3.12 : Amount-wise Classification of Term Sanctioned as on 31-03-1989

(Amount in Rs. 000's)

	No.	*Amount*
Loans upto Rs. 10000	8041	17154
Rs. 10001 to 25000	3907	72636
Rs. 25001 to 50000	4976	191864
Rs. 50001 to 100000	3624	269071
Rs. 100001 to 200000	6752	1104386
Rs. 200001 to 500000	6717	2031230
Rs. 500001 to 1000000	1800	1253664
Rs. 1000001 to 2000000	947	1397136
Rs.2000001 to 3000000	823	2003080

Sources : Reports of APSFC., Hyderabad.

Table 3.13 : Constitution-wise Classification of Term Loans Sanctioned (Effective) Disbursed and Outstanding As on 31-03-1989

(Amount Rs. 000's)

	Effective Sanctions		*Disburse-ment*	*Outsta-nding*
	No.	*Amount*	*Amount*	*Amount*
Public limited companies	185	126806	77607	145598
Private limited companies	1654	1852302	1488597	1565704
Co-operatives	36	6856	5488	3106
Partnership concerned	6318	2447232	2033346	881012
Joint Hindu family concerns	64	5578	3262	1930
Propertary concerns	22625	1528931	1170829	909010
Others (Societies)	11	3400	1461	4265
Total	**30893**	**5971105**	**4780590**	**3510625**

Source : Reports of A.P.S.F.C., Hyderabad.

An amount of Rs. 59,711.05 lakhs has been sanctioned so for to 30,893 units up to 31.3.1989, out of which an amount of Rs. 47,805 lakhs only has been disbursed and Rs. 35,106.25 lakhs is net outstanding as on 31.3.1989. Thus small-scale units occupy a predominant place in the lending patterns and financial assistance to industrial units, both in terms of number and also in number sanctioned by the Corporation.

Notes :

1. APSFC Annual Reports for the years 1984-85, 1985-86 and 1986-87, Hyderabad.

4

Promotion of Small-Scale Industries

We have already discussed the various activities of the Andhra Pradesh State Financial Corporation in Andhra Pradesh in Chapter 3. Now we shall move forward and discuss in detail the number of activities of the Corporation in the direction of financing industrial units in Anantapur District. As stated already, the detailed discussions on the activities of financing of industries by Andhra Pradesh State Financial Corporation will be confined to Anantapur district on though we have discussed in general fashion the entire gamut of the activities of the Andhra Pradesh State Financial Corporation in an earlier chapter. An earnest attempt is made in the following paragraphs to analyse and appraise the diversity of the activities of the Corporation in Anantapur district, in which the office (branch office) of Andhra Pradesh State Financial Corporation started from 1.8.1980.

Contribution to Small-Scale Industries by APSFC

Table 4.1 shows that during the years 1984-85, 1987-88 and 1988-89 the Corporation has financed all the small-scale industries that are established in Anantapur district. During the year 1985-86 the Corporation has financed to 97.63 per

Table 4.1 : Comparative Study of Industrial Units Year-wise Assistance by A.P.S.F.C. during 1984–89 in Anantapur District

Year	*Total Units*	*Small-Scale Units*	*Percentage of Small Scale Units*
1984–85	123	123	100.00
1985–86	169	165	97.63
1986–87	258	250	96.90
1987–88	485	485	100.00
1988–89	507	507	100.00
As on 31st March, 1989	2133	2094	98.17

Source : *Reports of A.P.S.F.C.*, Branch Office, Anantapur.

cent (i.e. 165 out of 169 units) that were started in this district. But in the year 1986-87 only 250 out of 258 units got the financial assistance from the Corporation.

A glance at the figures in Table 4.2. reveals as to how the Corporation has been stepping up its activities of financing for small-scale industries year after year gradually. Another remarkable feature which should necessarily invite out attention is the fact of intensifying of the financing activities from 1984-85 onwards only though some sort of activities was undertaken in this direction right from the inception of Corporation.

Up to the end of March, 1989 a total amount of Rs. 3,073.41 lakhs has been sanctioned (effective) as loans to the 2,044 small-scale industrial units. Out of this amount, actually an amount of Rs. 2,095.23 lakhs was disbursed. An amount of Rs. 1,410.17 lakhs has been shown an outstanding as on 31.3.1989.

This may perhaps be due to the shift in the policies of the Government of India as well as the State Government policies in the matter of promotion of small-scale industries with vigorous enthusiasm and redoubled spirit. Besides, the

Table 4.2 : Loans Sanctioned, Disbursed during 1984 to 1989 and as on 31st March in Anantapur District

(Amount in Rs. '000)

Year	*Sanctions*		*Disbursement*
	No.	Amount	amount
1984–85	123	28819	21341
1985–86	165	39776	20568
1986–87	258	47301	28449
1987–88	485	61914	40302
1988–89	507	80016	49383
As on 31st March, 1989	2044	307341	209523

Source : *Reports of A.P.S.F.C.*, Branch Office, Anantapur.

policy of the Government to develop industrialization in the backward areas with an object of achieving the ultimate goal of regional balanced development of the economy and industrializations in particular, announced in the various five years plans of the Government of India, is one of the important reasons for this remarkable shift, trend and pattern of sanctioning loans by the Corporation. Another factor which contributed in a substantial manner for the tremendous increase in the amount of loans sanctioned and disbursed to various industrial units in Anantapur district in recent years (i.e. from 1984-85 onwards) is the general tempo of rapid economic development in the country and in Andhra Pradesh particularly. What is the Corporation has done during the last 34 years in regard the industrial financing in Anantapur district is indeed very gratifying.

It can be observed from the Table 4.3 that the maximum number (1031) of effective sanctions of loans have been made in the range of Rs. 25,001 to Rs. 50,000 closely followed by loans in the range of Rs. 2,00,001 to 5,00,000 (771) and in the range of Rs. 1,00,001 to Rs. 2,00,000 (126) sharing the third rank respectively. This order of ranking is purely in terms of the number of units for which loans are sanctioned. But if we

Table 4.3 : Amount-wise Distribution of Loans Sanctioned by A.P.S.F.C. as on 31st March, 1989 in Anantapur District

(Amount in Rs. '000)

Amount (Rs.)	*Gross Sanctions 1987–88*		*Gross Sanctions 1988–89*		*Effective Sanctions since inception*	
	No.	*Amt.*	*No.*	*Amt.*	*No.*	*Amt.*
Upto 10000	—	—	1	10	9	92
10001–25000	7	131	20	279	56	1120
25001–50000	262	11738	217	10046	1031	47427
50001–100000	19	1599	12	860	65	5576
100001–200000	29	4290	28	4390	126	22152
200001–500000	161	39804	220	58750	771	338937
500001–750000	7	4352	9	5681	25	16995
Above 7,50,000	—	—	—	—	—	—
Total	185	61914	507	80016	2083*	432299*

Note : * Refers to all units including small-scale units.

Source : Reports of A.P.S.F.C., Branch Office, Anantapur.

are to take the order of ranking in terms of the total amount of loans sanctioned in any particular range, loans in the range of Rs. 2,00,001 to Rs. 5,00,000 occupy the first place with an amount of 3,389.37 lakhs to 771 units followed by loans in the rang of Rs. 25,001 to Rs. 50,000 to 1031 units amounting to Rs. 474.27 lakhs and loans in the range of Rs. 1,00,001 to Rs. 2,00,000 to 126 units for an amount of 221.52 lakhs. The above analysis is confined to the figures upto the end of March, 1989. This is the same for analysis of the figures of years 1987-88, 1988-89 respectively except in the terms of position of number of loans during 1988-89, because in 1988-89, the number of loans (220) stood first in the range of Rs. 2,00,001 to Rs. 5,00,000. An interesting feature, that can be observed from the various particulars furnished in the Table 4.3 is that small amounts of loans (not necessarily very small for example up to Rs. 50,000) are sanctioned to a large number of units by the Corporation. Another fact which should draw our attention in this context is that very large amounts (Rs. 5 lakhs and above) are paid to very few persons (25) as on 31st March, 1989.

Loan Assistance to Different Small-Scale Industries

Particulars of the industry-wise break up of the loan assistance by the Corporation have been given in Table 4.4. As can be observed from the various figures in Table 4.4. that transport industry has bagged the largest amount of assistance from the Corporation (896 units have received Rs. 1,018.61 lakhs) since its inception. Transport industries group occupies the first place both in terms of number of units as well as the amount sanctioned. Engineering group of industries occupy the second place in the order of raking in our industry-wise break up analysis of loan assistance by the Corporation. As on 31st March, 1989. 282 units of this group

Table 4.4 : Industry-wise Break-up of Assistance given by A.P.S.F.C. in Anantapur District as on 31st March, 1989

(Amount in Rs. '000)

Sl.	*Items*	*Effective Sanctions*	
		No.	*Amount*
1.	Food Products	194	17848
2.	Jute and Textile	74	45369
3.	Non-metallic industry	306	38072
4.	Engineering industry	282	49372
5.	Chemical and chemical products	59	19093
6.	Printing and paper products	98	29155
7.	Furniture and wood products	86	3554
8.	Hotel industry	22	1466
9.	Transport industry	896	101861
10.	Miscellaneous	27	1551
	Total	**2044**	**307341**

Source : *Reports of A.P.S.F.C.*, Branch Office, Anantapur.

received a total amount of assistance of Rs. 493.72 lakhs. Next comes jute and textile group of industries. 74 units in this group received Rs. 453.69 lakhs. It is obvious from the analysis in Table 4.4 that hotel industry received the least amount of assistance from the Corporation. 22 units in this group have received a total amount of Rs. 14.66 lakhs. This will reflect on the poor response of this group of industries to the assistance offered by the Corporation. It may indicate of the other sources of financing of these industrial groups.

As can be seen from the particulars of the amounts of loans sanctioned upto 31st March, 1989, given in Table 4.5, the Corporation has assisted the largest number of sole proprietary concerns (1562) followed by partnership concerns (465) and private limited companies (8) and public limited companies (6) and co-operative institutions (3). This order of ranging of financial assistance is rendered to the various industrial units constitution-wise in terms of numbers (of units financed) and in terms of amounts. But if we would like to analyse the same date in terms of the amounts of loans sanctioned, constitution wise, sole proprietary concerns bagged the largest amount of assistance (1562 units have received Rs. 1749.44 lakhs) followed by partnership

Table 4.5 : Constitution-wise Distribution of Industrial Units which received General Assistance from A.P.S.F.C. upto 31–03–98 in Anantapur District

(Amount in Rs. '000)

Sl. No.	*Item*	*Effective Sanctions*		*Disbursement*
		No.	*Amount*	
1.	Public Ltd. Company	6	35575	19329
2.	Private Ltd. Company	8	27931	19973
3.	Co-operative Sector	3	1465	1172
4.	Partnership concerns	465	65426	53592
5.	Sole Proprietory concerns	1562	174944	130586
	Total	**2044**	**307341**	**224652**

Source : *Reports of A.P.S.F.C.*, Branch Office, Anantapur.

concerns (465 units received Rs. 674.26 lakhs) and public limited company concerns taking of third place (6 units received Rs. 355.75 lakhs). Both in terms of numbers and amount of assistance sanctioned, public limited companies, private limited companies and co-operative concerns are shown a step motherly treatment. This is not any accusation against the Corporation, but this fact suggests of the existence of other source of financing for these three types of institutions. There are a number of co-operative organisations at the State and National levels ready to offer financial assistance to the co-operative institutions. Similarly, there are a large number of corporations and special financial institutions set-up by the Central and State Governments (for example IFC, ICIC, IDBI etc.) to look after the needs of the finance for these public limited companies which are comparatively of a large size.

Year-wise Analysis of Arrears

Table 4.6 reveals that the particulars of arrears (principal and interest) due for recovery by the Corporation (year-wise analysis of the amount of arrears to be recovered by the Corporation) is amounting up from year to year. One need not get depressed by the figures of arrears, swelling year after

Table 4.6 : Year-wise (Cumulative) Arrears from 1984–85 to 1988–89 in Anantapur District

(Amount in Rs. '000)

As on 31st March of every year	*No.*	*Amount of principal and interest in arrears*
1985	167	5564
1986	169	6929
1987	192	4277
1988	279	9554
1989	390	15902

Source : *Reports of A.P.S.F.C.*, Branch Office, Anantapur.

year. This is partly due to increase in the amount of loans sanctioned and disbursed in these years. It is but natural that along with the stepping up of the level of assistance by the Corporation the amounts of arrears also will increase. There is nothing particularly to worry about seriously over this issue as the Corporation has already taken all the needed measures in the direction by collecting its dues from its borrowers/customers (industrial units).

Age-wise Analysis of Arrears

As can be seen from the particulars of the age-wise analysis of arrears due to be recovered by the Corporation up to 31.3.1989, a total amount of Rs. 159.02 lakhs has to be recovered by the Corporation from it its borrowers. Out of this amount, the amounts of arrears which are long overdue (7 years and above) are of a very limited magnitude viz. Rs. 2.91 lakhs. This forms hardly 1.8 per cent of the total amount of arrears to be collected. This reflects partly on the efficiency of the collection drive of the Corporation. This will also reflect partly on the fact that there is no need to be seriously concerned about the arrears position of the Corporation. Most of the amounts of the arrears are within a range of 6 to 12 and 12 to 24 months. By any stretch of imagination, this cannot be considered as overdues. The conclusion we can draw very safely from the analysis of data from Table 4.7 is that the Corporation's staff has been very efficiently conducting the arrears collection campaign.

Industry-wise Analysis of Arrears

If we analyse the particulars of arrears as on 31st March, 1989 in Anantapur district due from different industrial units belonging to different groups of industries was mentioned in Table 4.8, it can be noticed that the industrial units in the transport industry group owe the largest amount to the Corporation Rs. 50.71 lakhs. It is but natural that the transport group of industries which have received the largest total amount of loans from the Corporation should also pay a very

Table 4.7 : Particulars of Arrears (Age-wise) as on 31–03–89 in Anantapur District

(Amount in Rs. '000)

Age of arrears	*No.*	*Amount of principal and interest in arrears*	*Percentage of total arrears*
0–3 months	57	1816	11.42
3–6 months	59	2217	13.94
6–12 months	72	3893	24.48
12–24 months	92	2826	17.77
24–48 months	39	2061	12.96
4–5 years	42	2124	13.36
5–7 years	21	674	4.24
7 years above	8	291	1.83
Total	**390**	**15902**	**100.00**

Source : *Reports of A.P.S.F.C.*, Branch Office, Anantapur.

Table 4.8 : Particulars of the Industry-wise Arrears as on 31st March, 1989 to be recovered by the Corporation in Anantapur District

(Amount in Rs. '000)

Sl. No.	*Name of the Industry*	*No.*	*Amount of principal and interest in arrears*
1.	Food products	35	1989
2.	Jute and Textiles	10	2342
3.	Non-metallic industry	56	1012
4.	Chemical and chemical products	10	972
5.	Printing and paper industry	17	1558
6.	Furniture and wood products	14	228
7.	Engineering industry	52	2535
8.	Hotel industry	4	74
9.	Transport industry	185	5071
10.	Miscellaneous industry	7	121
	Total	**390**	**15902**

Source · Reports of A.P.S.F.C., Branch Office, Anantapur.

large amount of arrears. Engineering industrial group take the second place in the order of ranking of arrears. The third place goes to Jute and Textile industries group with a sum of Rs. 23.42 lakhs to be recovered from them. Engineering industries group and jute and textile industries group which occupy the II and III place in the matter of total amount of loans sanctioned and disbursed by the Corporation, are taking of the II and III place again in the matter of arrears to be recovered from them respectively. This is purely a strange coincidence of taking the same rank both in the matter of sanctions of loans and also arrears to be recovered.

Composite Loan Scheme

Up to the end of 31st March, 1989 a total amount of Rs. 239.97 lakhs has been sanctioned to 684 small-scale industries units under the Composite Loan Scheme. Out of which, an amount of Rs. 57.32 lakhs only has been actually disbursed under this scheme. This scheme is comparatively of a recent origin. The composite plan scheme was introduced for the first time in the year 1979-80. and 16 small industrial units have been sanctioned loan as assistance of Rs. 4 lakhs in the very first 3 months of its implementation. We find a gradual stepping up of the loan assistance by the Corporation under this scheme year after year. In the year 1984-85, 25 units received Rs. 6.25 lakhs in the next year 1985-86, 26 units received Rs. 6.50 lakhs and in subsequent years 1986-87 and 1987-88, 92 units received Rs. 27.15 lakhs and 248 units received Rs. 112.94 lakhs respectively. These figures will reveal as to how the Corporation is taking increasing interest in the implementation of the composite loans scheme in order to assist effectively the small-scale industrial units in the rural areas. This also reflects upon the growing interest of the Corporation in the development of rural industrialisation and participation in the Government of India's and Andhra Pradesh State Government's integrated rural development projects and generation of additional employment opportunities in the rural areas. A more vigorous implementation of this scheme will go a long way in translating the dreams, ambitions, aspirations hopes, plans, programmes and schemes of the Government at the Centre and in the State into action oriented programmes and promoting rural welfare.

What is expiained in Table 4.9 is a total picture of situation of the composite loans sanctioned by the Corporation. But in Table 4.10 the industry wise distribution analysis of composite loans sanctioned (effective) by the Corporation in Anantapur district up to 32.3.1989 are provided. The non-metallic group of small-scale industrial units bagged the largest amount of assistance under this programme. 230 units in the non-metallic group have been sanctioned loan assistance of Rs. 84.80 lakhs up to the end of 31.3. 1989. The second place goes to general engineering industry group, 152 units in this group have been sanctioned loan assistance of Rs. 52.32 lakhs till the end of March, 1989. Third place is occupied by food products group with a loan assistance of Rs. 43.68 lakhs to 127 units. Printing and paper products and hotel industry group received the least amount of assistance under this scheme. Only 14 printing and paper industrial units have been sanctioned Rs. 4.84 lakhs under this scheme. Similarly hotel industry also did not receive any satisfactory

Table 4.9 : Composite Loans sanctioned and Disbursed in Anantapur District during 1984–89 and as on 31–03–1989

(Amount in Rs. '000)

Year	*Sanctions*		*Disbursement*
	No.	Amount	amount
1984–85	25	625	554
1985–86	26	650	496
1986–87	92	2751	18
1987–88	248	11294	304
1988–89	166	7157	141
As on 31st March, 1989	684	23997	5732

Source : *Reports of A.P.S.F.C.*, Branch Office, Anantapur.

Table 4.10 : Industry-wise Particulars of Composite Loans Sanctioned, Disbursed and Outstanding in Anantapur District as on 31–03–1989

(Amount in Rs. '000)

Sl. No.	*Name of the Industry*	*Effective Sanctions*		*Disbursement Amount*	*Outstanding Amount*
		No.	Amt.		
1.	Food Products	127	4368	1426	1230
2.	Jute and Textile	66	2271	786	698
3.	Non-metallic industry	230	8480	2122	1896
4.	Engineering industry	152	5232	943	843
5.	Chemcial and chemcial products	40	1020	267	208
6.	Paper and Printing industry	14	484	26	25
7.	Furniture and wood products	42	1590	126	98
8.	Hotel industry	13	552	36	32
9.	Transport industry	—	—	—	—
	Total	**684**	**23997**	**5732**	**5030**

Source : *Reports of A.P.S.F.C.*, Branch Office, Anantapur.

encouragement or assistance under this programme. Only 13 hotel industrial units received a total amount of assistance of Rs. 5.52 lakhs. The reasons for the very negligible amount of assistance extended to these two groups of industrial units (printing and paper products and hotel industry) are obvious. There is not so much entrepreneurship or market for the products in the rural areas. The technical know-how in the rural areas for these two groups of industries is also very limited and hence the very small amounts of loan assistance provided to these units.

State of Working of the Industrial Units Financed by the Corporation in Anantapur District: An Appraisal

Out of the 2044 (industrial units for which financial assistance has been sanctioned and disbursed by the Corporation (excluding the units for which accounts are already closed) up to the end of 31st March, 1989, 140 units are still in construction stage, 300 units are in installation stage, 803 units have just recently commenced their production operations, 369 units are in a well established stage and running on their operations well, 108 units are in limping stage and 324 units are to be either sick or closed.

If we take up our analysis industry group wise as mentioned in the Table 4.11, in the food products industry group, 21 units which are in construction stage; 32 units in the installation stage, 58 units have just commenced their operation; 42 units are running well, 11 units are limping and 30 units are either sick or closed.

In the Jute and Textile group, 11 units are in the construction stage, 9 units are in installation stage; 23 units have just commenced the production; 18 units are well with their running operations; 4 units are limping and 9 units are declared sick.

In the non-metallic industry group; 35 units are still in construction stage; 49 units are in installation stage; 92 units have just commenced their production operations; 54 units are running well; 16 units are limping and 60 units are declared sick.

In the Engineering industry, 6 units are in production stage; 106 units have been in the installation stage; 64 units have just commenced their production; 36 units are in a well established stage with a satisfactory running of their operations; 12 units are limping and 58 units are declared either sick or closed.

In the chemical and chemical products industries group 11 units are still in the construction stage, 12 units are in the erection stage, 8 units have just commenced their production operations; 12 units are in a fairly satisfactory working condition; 7 units are limping and 9 units are declared either sick or closed.

Table 4.11 State of Working of Small-scale Units Assisted by Corporation in Anantapur District as on 31st March, 1989

Sl. No.	Name of the Industry	Installation stage	Construction stage	Commencing production	Well established good in operations	Limping stage	Sick/ closed	Total
1.	Food Products	32	21	58	42	11	30	194
2.	Jute and Textile	9	11	23	18	4	9	74
3.	Non-metallic industry	49	35	92	54	16	60	306
4.	Engineering industry	106	6	64	36	12	58	282
5.	Chemical and chemical products	12	11	8	12	7	9	59
6.	Printing and paper industry	—	18	30	40	8	2	98
7.	Furniture and Wood industry	26	—	30	22	8	—	86
8.	Hotel industry	—	3	12	7	—	—	22
9.	Transport industry	62	28	480	132	40	1154	896
10.	Miscellaneous products	4	7	6	6	2	2	27
	Total	**300**	**140**	**803**	**369**	**108**	**324**	**2044**

Source : Reports of A.P.S.F.C., Branch office, Anantapur.

In the printing and paper products industry group 18 units are in construction stage; 30 units have just commenced their production operations; 40 units are well with their production operations; 8 units are limping and only 2 units are sick.

In the furniture and wood products group, 26 units are in installation stage;, 30 units have commenced their production operations; 22 units are in a fairly satisfactory working condition; 8 units are limping and no unit finds either sick or closed.

In the hotel industry group 3 units are in construction stage, 12 units have just commenced their production operations, 7 units are well with their production operations and no limping and sick. The latest reports on the working of the hotel indicate that it is progressing in a fairly satisfactory manner and may be able to reach its goal of prosperity soon.

In the transport industries group, 28 units are in construction stage, 62 units are in installation stage, 480 units have just commenced their production operations, 132 units are well established and running their operations on a commercial scale, 40 units are limping and 154 units are sick.

In the miscellaneous products group out of 27 units which have been sanctioned financial assistance, 7 units are in production stage; 4 units are in erection stage; 6 units have just commenced their production operations; 6 units are well with their production operations; 2 units are limping and 2 units are declared either sick or closed.

On an overall evaluation of the working of the various industrial units for which financial assistance has been provided by the Andhra Pradesh State Financial Corporation, a revelation that come to the mind of any observer is that of about 324 units, only one has declared either sick or closed. Among the remaining 1720 units another 108 units have been limping and several, units are either in the construction stage or installation stage or have just commenced their production operations. The number of all such units will total upto 1620. That means it may be too early, rather hasty, ill-conceived or pre-mature to pass any judgement on their working as they have not seen the light of the day so far. Hardly 369 units are reported to be running in a satisfactory condition. This does not speak well of the state of affairs of the industrial units assisted by the Corporation and it is perhaps due to the delays in construction, erection or installation or fulfilling the various formalities in the formative stage, 440 units have not started with their programmes of production. Among the rest of the units also, several of them have been observed to be encountering some difficulty or other and are not able to get one well with their plans of production and sales etc.

5

Summary of Findings and Suggestions

The most pressing need of developing countries is rapid industrialisation for achieving the basic objectives of their economic and social progress, especially hike in per capita income. So industrial development is an effort in which the developing countries place a major hope of finding a solution to their problems of poverty, security, and over population and ending their newly realised backwardness in the modern world.

In this regard the contribution of small-scale sector to industrial development assumes vital importance in the context of developing Indian economy. The development of small-scale industries is not only crucial for accelerating industrial growth but also for achieving the social objectives of disposal of industry and equitable distribution of wealth.

For the above said purpose the official policy encourages the growth of small-scale industries in India. Nearly 1,00,000 new units enter this sector every year. There were as many as 15.92 lakh small-scale units in 1987-88 accounting for 35 per cent of the gross industrial production and quarter of the country's exports. Over one crore persons are employed in this sector which produces a wide range of goods worth of Rs. 64,500 crores. The development and growth of the Indian small-scale sector is the envy of many a third world country.

The availability of finance might be the most important determinant in tne establishment and growth of small manufacturing enterprises. It is ironical that small-scale industrial sector which now contributes more than 40 per cent of the industrial output, has been provided with just only 11 per cent of the total credit sanctioned by commercial banks. Even now many small industrial units are depending on non-institutional sources for their financial requirements. Government of India and State Government recognised the need for specialised financial and developmental institutions and set on the task of building up a net-work of such institutions like Andhra Pradesh State Financial Corporation.

In case of Andhra Pradesh, the small-scale industrial sector has not registered an appreciable rate of growth in some regions, especially in a backward region like Rayalaseema owing to lack of development finance. The declining trend in the growth of small-scale industrial sector in a backward district like Anantapur of Rayalaseema region is mainly because of financial constraint.

Since industrial development of a place largely depends on the availability of finance and availability of resources-both human and physical, a detailed survey of resource-base of Anantapur district has been attempted in Chapter 2. Anantapur district, of Rayalaseema region, is one of the 25 districts of Andhra Pradesh and lies between 13-40' and 15-15' northern latitude and 76-50' and 78-30' eastern longitude. According to 1981 census, Anantapur district had a population of 25.48 lakhs. The total geographical area of the District is 19,125 sq. km. The District is less densely populated with a density of population 133 per sq. km. as against 196 for the State as a whole of the total population.

The District has three distinct and natural divisions. To impart the necessary skills to the people, the District has a number of educational institutions both for general education and technical education. Further, 50 per cent of the total number of the unemployed in the District are educated. Thus, the District has adequate human resources, both skilled and unskilled, willing and capable of working in industries. The non-human resources that are available within the District comprise the agricultural and mineral resources along with forest wealth and live-stock.

Since Anantapur district is one of the twelve industrially backward districts of Andhra Pradesh, identified by the Union Government, monetary concessions and fiscal incentives are available to entrepreneurs who set up industries in the District. Further, as one of the three districts selected by the Andhra Pradesh Government for 'Intensive Industrial Development' entrepreneurs of Anantapur district are eligible for special concessions in respect of power tariff, water tariff and tax concessions. Land for industrial use is also made available free of cost upto a specified limit.

Availability of required resources in a fair measure coupled with infrastructural facilities make Anantapur district suitable for undertaking industrialisation. The policies of Balanced Regional Development and Development of Backward Areas, pursued by Government, also make Anantapur a fit place for undertaking industrial development

In view of the importance attached to the industrial development in Anantapur district, several programmes were envisaged by the Government for the development of the small-scale industry. In spite of these programmes, the problems confronting the growth of the sector are found unabated. Among all the problems, adequate and timely supply of credit seems to be more serious than any other problem. There were a large number of agencies concerned with the development of small-scale industries. Many of the central and State level organisation had their own functionaries working at the district levels, and they tended to operate individually with no contact with each other. The proliferated schemes, agencies and organisations confused small entrepreneurs. The procedures for availing the assistance from the developmental agencies were cumbersome and bewildered many a small entrepreneur who had nowhere to go to solve their problems. Thus process of promotion and development of industries in Anantapur District has not been an easy one.

Andhra Pradesh State Financial Corporation is the major agency to deal with the financial requirement of small industries at the district level itself.

The present study tries to analyse the assistance provided by Andhra Pradesh State Financial Corporation for the promotion of small industries in Andhra Pradesh and in Anantapur district in third and fourth chapters respectively.

The Andhra Pradesh State Financial Corporation has been engaged continuously during the last 34 years of it's existence in promoting the cause of rapid industrial development in Andhra Pradesh. Inspite of some short-comings in the functioning, organisation, management and administration of the Corporation, the Andhra Pradesh State Financial Corporation has rendered a signal service to the cause of development of small-scale industries in Andhra Pradesh and particularly in the backward regions like Rayalaseema. The contribution of the Andhra Pradesh State Financial Corporation to the cause of small-scale industrial development in a drought prone and backward district like Anantapur is indeed a considerable one.

The main objective of the Andhra Pradesh State Financial Corporation is to meet the unfulfilled term credit needs of medium and small-scale industrial concerns located in the state of Andhra Pradesh. In order to achieve its objectives, the Corporation has been operating various schemes keeping in view the changing needs of wide range of entrepreneurs to make financial assistance available for establishing industrial ventures.

Andhra Pradesh State Financial Corporation, although,

was operating various schemes to assist small-scale units, no scheme other than the provision of term finance for the acquisition of fixed assets was popular among the many units. The above discussion indicates that though there were various schemes in operation but very few schemes are known to all.

In order to serve entrepreneurs effectively nearer to the place of operation, the Andhra Pradesh State Financial Corporation has laid much emphasis on branch expansion programme. Under the branch expansion programme of the Corporation, seven new branch offices have been established during 1984-85 taking the total number of branch offices to 20 in addition to 5 fields office. There is a need to strengthen the branch offices.

The Andhra Pradesh State Financial Corporation has so far sanctioned term loans to the tune of Rs. 88,210.36 lakhs to 32243 units upto 31st March, 1989 in Andhra Pradesh. In Rayalaseema region alone it has sanctioned a financial assistance of a magnitude of Rs. 10050.26 lakhs till the end of March, 1989. In Anantapur District loans for an amount Rs. 3,073.41 lakhs have been sanctioned to 2044 units upto 31st March, 1989 and out of which Rs. 4,095.23 been disbursed.

Some entrepreneurs, though they were in need of term finance and were aware of the facilities from Andhra Pradesh State Financial Corporation, they did not approach the Agency due to their fear that they might not be able to comply with procedural formalities. This indicates the bureaucratic setup prevailing in Andhra Pradesh State Financial Corporation.

Twenty per cent of the units, which applied for loans were denied of loans by Andhra Pradesh State Financial Corporation for two reasons viz., (i) lack of proper supporting information and (ii) inability to produce guarantee due to inherent weaknesses of the entrepreneurs such as lack of proper industrial background, lack of awareness of the managerial techniques. They were not able to provide the required information.

Andhra Pradesh State Financial Corporation took more than six months for the sanction of the loans in case of 62 per cent of the units. And in the case of 30.28 per cent of the units, it took more than eight months for the release of funds. It indicates the inordinate delays made in the sanctioning and releasing the loan amount by Andhra Pradesh State Financial Corporation.

A variety of special schemes have also been implemented for promoting the cause of industrial development in Anantapur District by Andhra Pradesh State Financial Corporation. In addition to this, Rs. 239.97 lakhs has been sanctioned to 684 units under composite loan scheme to promote the cause of Rural Development Programme. The Corporation has also provided a variety of other service to several small-scale industrial units.

Food processing, Jute and Textile, non-metallic, chemical and chemical products, printing and paper, furniture and wood products, Engineering, Hotel, and Transport etc., are some of the groups of industrial units assisted by the Andhra Pradesh State Financial Corporation in Anantapur District.

The Andhra Pradesh State Financial Corporation has improved its performance, organisational and management to considerable extent during the set-up last three decades of its existence. It has simplified its procedures, it has done away with guarantees for loans for small units (upto Rs. 3 lakhs). It has dispensed with legal mortgage expenses in respect of small-scale industries. The Andhra Pradesh State Financial Corporation has also been providing financial assistance to industrial units in backward areas at subsidised rates of interest.

All is not well with the functioning of the Corporation. Despite the fact that it has made considerable progress, it seems a lot of gaps are yet to be filled up, a large number of deficiencies in its functioning, performance, organisation and administration have yet to be removed. It can spread its net of financial assistance to industrial units, particularly small-scale industrial units in Andhra Pradesh, still wider. It can enlarge its frame-work of assistance for the industrial development in backward districts like Anantapur stil' further.

Suggestions

In order to tone up the administrative mechanism for financing the small and medium-scale industries by the Andhra Pradesh State Finance Corporation and also to place the units assisted by the Corporation on a viable footing, the following suggestions are given. It is the firm opinion of the researcher that when these suggestions are implemented in letter and spirit, the Andhra Pradesh State Financial Corporation can render more useful, effective, meaningful and fruitful service in the cause of industrial development in Anantapur District. Of course, whatever help is extended by the Andhra Pradesh State Financial Corporation to the small and medium-scale industries, there is no guarantee that they will be developed fully. We have to remember the important fact that, Andhra Pradesh State Financial Corporation is one of the several institutions or organisations engaged in assisting and promoting industrial development in Anantapur District. The entire responsibility for the industrial development in Anantapur District cannot be thrust on the Andhra Pradesh State Financial Corporation alone.

The following suggestions will enable the Andhra Pradesh State Financial Corporation to revitalise its functioning and contribute its mite in the achievement of the ultimate goal of rapid industrialisation in Anantapur District.

(i) The State Government and Industrial Development Bank of India should provide funds to the Andhra Pradesh State Financial Corporation enabling it to render more effective financial assistance to the needy units. The State Government and Industrial Development Bank authorities should adopt a more liberal, flexible and pragmatic approach and attitude towards the whole problem.

(2) The Andhra Pradesh State Financial Corporation should try to mobilise more resources by attracting more and more deposits from the public rather than depending excessively on the State Government or the IDBI for refinancing facilities.

(3) Adequate power must be delegated to the branch managers. This will help in avoiding delays in decision making and in avoiding bureaucratic delays ending red-tapism and facilitating speedy disposal of loan applications.

(4) In order to strengthen the branch office in all aspects-technical, managerial, administrative, financial consultative etc., adequate number of persons with the required qualifications, experiences, knowledge expertise, proficiency and high level of skills in various branches of accounting, auditing, cost accounting, financial controls, technological, scientific and engineering mater etc., should be appointed. Project appraisal work, field studies etc., can be conducted than more effectively, instead of running here and there for advice, guidance and counselling etc., as is done now. The branch offices should be equipped with a full complement of staff with a diversity of skills and experience etc. This will speed up the processing of loan applications and also hasten the process of disbursements and loan recoveries etc. The field investigation staff should be enlarged.

(5) The State Government should adequately ensure that all the needed infrastructural facilities are provided to the industrial units, set up with the financial assistance of the Corporation; otherwise, whatever help the Corporation extends to the industrial units, will go to waste.

(6) It is also suggested that the Corporation's officials should get into touch with the various other Government officials, so that they can render better service to the industrial units assisted by it. It is true that some

efforts are made in this direction even now by the Corporation's officials. But what is to be done now is that their efforts have to be intensified further.

(7) Several Schemes introduced by Andhra Pradesh State Financial Corporation but are not known to many entrepreneurs. It is to enough if a scheme is introduced. It must be known to the people for whom it is meant. Otherwise, the scheme would become an obsolete. For this purpose widen publicity must be given for various schemes in operation through mass media - T.V., radios, new papers, cinema etc. At the same time, window display can be made at all important places where the public gathers normally. But the places chosen for this purpose may be those where industrialists and businessmen assemble.

(8) All types of units which are eligible for guarantee facilities under Reserve Bank of India's credit guarantee scheme are to be brought under the scope of Andhra Pradesh State Financial Corporation's loan operation.

(9) Terms and conditions for any loan must be simple, specific and understandable even to a layman. Ambiguous and complicated rules are to be deleted. The Andhra Pradesh State Financial Corporation has to provide assistance for the entrepreneurs at all stages till the disbursement of loan is over.

(10) Andhra Pradesh State Financial Corporation has to avoid the practice of asking for third party guarantee as the assets are to be pledged until the loan amount is cleared off completely. Same practice may be adopted by the institutions which provide term loans.

(11) Andhra Pradesh State Financial Corporation makes inordinate delays. The provisions of credit must not only be adequate but also timely. All the institutional agencies like Andhra Pradesh State Financial Corporation must taken note of the importance of timely supply

of credit and should sanction and release funds within short period.

(12) State Financial Corporations and commercial banks can have co-ordination in sanctioning of loans. As it is noticed in the present study, many units are securing term loans from Andhra Pradesh State Financial Corporation and working capital loans from commercial banks. In those cases, scrutiny of the application of a particular unit is being made twice. Instead of this, by forming coordinated committee with the representatives of both banks and Andhra Pradesh State Financial Corporation, the application can be scrutinized jointly. This will reduce undue delays in sanctioning loans.

(13) In the days of growing inflation, the price of machinery and equipment tend to rise. Resultantly, the credit requirement may not be the same if considerable time is taken in processing, sanctioning and disbursing the loans. So provision may also be made for price escalation so that any change in price structure may automatically be adjusted without the need for revised estimates. Same is the case with the assessment of working capital.

(14) At every stage i.e., percentage of amount sanctioned as a percentage of amount applied, time lag between date of application and date of sanctioned and of release of funds, and rate of refusal etc., the procedure must be simplified and action expedited. Smaller units, units of the proprietory concerns and units belonging to rural areas were much affected in securing loans from Andhra Pradesh State Financial Corporation. This is much contrary to the objectives of Government for dispersal of industries and balanced regional development. This is possible only when Andhra Pradesh State Financial Corporation can provide loans to all categories of Units without being influenced by their size, location, security or the position of the entrepreneur.

(15) The branch manager may be empowered to sanction loans upto Rs. One lakhs without waiting for the approval and sanction from the Head Office.

(16) Loan upto Rs. 50,000/- to small sector should be sanctioned as composite loan whether it is equipment finance or working capital or both. Such loan should have repayment period or 7 to 10 years even more considering the small amount of surpluses which can be expected to be generated and the continuous essential need of the borrowers.

To conclude, much is said about the role of Andhra Pradesh State Financial Corporation in the Development of small industries. In reality it is not so because of the multiplicity of rules and regulations, duplicating procedures, absence of co-ordinated efforts and inordinate delays. Unless these constraints are cleared by the Andhra Pradesh State Financial Corporation through co-ordinated committees, the gigantic task of promoting small-scale industrialisation may not be accomplished.

Bibliography

Alexander, P.C., *Industrial Estates in India*, Bombay, Asia Publishing House, 1963.

Asian Productive Organisation, *Productivity through Consultation in Small Industrial Enterprise*, Tokyo, Imprint, 1974.

Balakrishna, G. *Financing of Small-Scale Industries in India*. Pune, Gokhale Institute of Politics and Economics, 1972.

Banks, Russell (Ed.), *Managing the Smaller Company*, Tarporewala Publishing Industries Pvt. Ltd., 1977.

Basu, S.K., *Place and Problems of Small Industries*, Calcutta, Mukherjee & Co., 1957.

Desai, Vasant, *Organisation and Management of Small-Scale Industries*, Himalaya Publishing House, Bombay, 1983.

Devenport Robert, W., *Financing the Small Manufacture in Developing Countries*, New York, Mc Graw Hill Book Company, 1967.

Dhar, P.N. & Lydall, H.F., *The Role of Small Enterprises in Indian Economic Development*. Asia Publishing House, Bombay, 1961.

Farooque, Q.H., *Small-Scale and Cottage Industries as a means of providing better opportunities for labour in India, Aligarh*, Muslim University, 1978.

Gopal Swaroop, *Advances to Small Industries and Small Borrowers*, New Delhi, Sultan Chand & Sons, 1970.

Holland Edward, D., *The Future of Small Business*, U.S.A. Frederick—A Prager, Inc. Publications, 1967.

Inderjit Singh & Gupta, N.S., *Financing of Small Industry*, New Delhi, S. Chand & Co. Limited, 1977.

Lokanatham, P.S., *Supply of Entrepreneurship and Technologists with Special Reference to East Asia*, London, Maxmillan & Company Limited, 1965.

Mathur, S.P., *Economics of Small-Scale Industries*, Delhi, Sundeep Prakashan, 1979.

Mehta, M.M., *Strucuture of Indian Industries*, Popular Book Depot, Bombay, 1956.

Menon, K.S.V., *Development of Backward Areas through Incentives*, New Delhi, Vidya Vahini, 1972.

Myrdal, Gunnar, *Asian Drama—An Enquiry into the Poverty of Nations*, London, Twentieth Century Fund, Inc., 1968.

Pareek, H.S., *Financing of Small-Scale Industry in a Developing Economy, New Delhi*, National Publishing House, 1978.

Ramakrishna, K.T., *Finances for Small-scale Industry in India*, Bombay, Asia Publishing House, 1962.

Rao, R.V., *Small Industries and the Developing Economy in India*, New Delhi, Concept Publishing House, 1979.

Ruddar Dutt and Sundaram, K.P.M., *Indian Economy*, S. Chand & Compnay (Pvt.) Limited, New Delhi, 1989.

Rondo Camaron and Patrick Hugh, T., "Introduction", *Banking in Early States of Industrialisation*, New York, Oxford University Press, 1967.

Satyanarayana, *Industrial Development in Backward Regions Resources and Planning*, Chugh Publications, Allahabad, 1989.

Sivayya, K.V. & Das, V.B.M., *Indian Industrial Economy*, S. Chand & Co., New Delhi, 1985.

Vepa Ram, K., *Small Industries in Seventies*, Delhi, Vikas Publications, 1971.

William Diamond, *Development Banks*, Baltimore. The Hopkins Press, 1957.

Periodicals

Chopra, Raksh, Financing of Small-Scale Industries, *Employment News*, Vol. XI, No. 25, 20th September, 1986.

Patnik, Uma Maheswar, Industrial Development in Andhra Pradesh—Need to Remedy Distortions, *Southern Economist*, Vol. 23, No. 2, May 15, 1989.

Prasad & Agarwal, "Industrialisation through Small-scale Sector", *The Indian Journal of Commerce*, Vol. XXXI, Part III, No. 116, September, 1978.

Patrick Hugh, T., "Financial Development and Economic Growth in Under-developed Countries", *Economic Development and Cultural Change*, Vol. XIX, No. 3, 1971.

Sharkar, M.C., Financing the New Entrepreneurs, *State Bank of India Monthly Review*, Vol. XIII, No. 6, June, 1974.

Sharma, R.A., "Entrepreneurial Motivation in India", *The Review of Commerce Studies*, Vol. III, 1974.

The Editor, Scope of Small-Scale Industry, *Employment News*. Vol. XI, No. 27, 4th October, 1986.

United Nations, New York, *Small Industry Bulletin for Asia and the Pacific*, No. 19, 1984.

Reports

Andhra Pradesh State Financial Corporation, *Role of Corporation in Effective of Small-Scale Industries—Report of the Working Group on Small-Scale Sector, Hyderabad,* 1986.

Andhra Pradesh State Financial Corporation, *Annual Reports, 1957 to 1989*, Head Office, Hyderabad.

Andhra Pradesh State Financial Corporation, *Annual Reports, 1981 to 1989*, Banch Office, Anantapur.

Bureau of Economics and Statistics Government of Andhra Pradesh, *Statistical Abstract of Andhra Pradesh*, Hyderabad, 1981.

Chief Planning Officer, "*Hand Book of Statistics—Anantapur District*", *1983–84*, Anantapur.

Department of Industries, Government of Andhra Pradesh, *Industrial Development in Anantapur District, Action Plan, 1983–84*, Hyderabad.

District Industries Centre, *Reports on Existing Industrial Estates and Industrial Development Areas in Anantapur District*, Anantapur, 1989.

Governmnt of Andhra Pradesh, *Hand Book of Statistics of Anantapur District*, Hyderabad, 1988.

Government of Andhra Pradesh, *Andhra Pradesh District Gazetteers, Anantapur*, Hyderabad, 1967.

Government of Andhra Pradesh, *Fifth Five Year Plan of Andhra Pradesh*, Hyderabad, 1973.

Government of Andhra Pradesh, *Seventh Five Year Plan of Andhra Pradesh*, Vol. I, Hyderabad, 1983.

Government of India, *Industrial Policy Resolution of 1948, 6th April, 1948*, As cited by *Small Industries in Seventies*, Vikas Publishing House, New Delhi, 1971.

Government of India, *Industrial Policy Resolution of 1956*, as cited by *Programmes of Industrial Development, 1956–61*, New Delhi, 1956.

Government of India, *Industrial Policy Resolution of 1977*, New Delhi, 23rd December, 1977.

Government of India Planning Commission, *First Five Year Plan*, New Delhi, 1952.

Government of India Planning Commission, *Second Five Year Plan*, New Delhi, 1956.

Government of India Planning Commission, *Third Five Year Plan*, New Delhi, 1960.

Government of India Planning Commission, *Fourth Five Year Plan*, New Delhi, 1969.

Government of India Planning Commission, *Draft Fifth Five Year Plan*, New Delhi, 1974.

Government of India Planning Commission, *Sixth Five Year Plan*, New Delhi, 1980.

Government of India Planning Commission, *Seventh Five Year Plan*, New Delhi, 1985.

International Bank for Reconstruction and Development, *Report on Small-Scale Industry in India, Vol. II*, London, 1972.

Office of the Employment Exchange, *A Report on the Educated, Unemployed of Anantapur District*, Anantapur, 1988.

Reserve Bank of India, *Report of working Group on Resource Mobilisation, Profitability etc., of State Finance Corporation*, Bombay, 1984.

United Nations Industrial Development Organisation, "*Financial Resources for Industrial Projects in Developing Countries", Third edition Industrial Investment and Financing Series, UNIDO, Vienna*, February, 1983.

Seminar

Reserve Bank of India, *Report of the Seminar on Financing of Small-Scale in India*, Bombay, 1987.

Dailies

The Economic Times (Bombay edition) dated 11th September, 1987.

The Financial Express (New Delhi edition) 20th September, 1986.

The Times of India (Bombay edition), dated 20th June, 1989.

The Financial Express (New Delhi edition), 24th July, 1987.

Index